GIFTED
GAMES™

NNAT® TEST PREP
for the NNAT2® / NNAT3® Level A and Level B

Gateway Gifted Resources™
www.GatewayGifted.com

PLEASE LEAVE US
A REVIEW!

Thank you for selecting this book. We are a family-owned publishing company - a consortium of educators, book designers, illustrators, parents, and kid-testers.

We would be thrilled if you left us a quick review on the website where you purchased this book!

The Gateway Gifted Resources™ Team
www.GatewayGifted.com

TABLE OF CONTENTS

INTRODUCTION

INTRODUCTION

ABOUT THIS BOOK -

This book helps prepare young learners for taking the NNAT2® / NNAT3® Level A and Level B.

THIS BOOK HAS 4 PARTS:

1. Introduction (p. 4-13):
- About This Book
- About The NNAT2® / NNAT3®
- Test-Taking Tips
- Practice Test Notes
- The Shape Detectives

The Shape Detectives

To increase child engagement and to add an incentive to complete book exercises, a detective theme accompanies this book. Read page 13 ("The Shape Detectives") together with your child. The book's characters belong to a detective agency. They want your child to help them solve "puzzles" (the exercises in the book) so that your child can join the detective agency, too! After your child completes the book, (s)he will "join" the Shape Detectives. However, feel free to modify as you see fit the number of pages/exercises your child must complete in order to receive his/her certificate. (The certificate for you to complete with your child's name is on page **96**.)

2. Practice Tests (p. 14-90)
The three practice tests included in this book provide:

- an opportunity for children to practice focusing on a group of questions for a longer time period (something to which most children are not accustomed)
- a way for parents to identify points of strength and weakness among the test question types

These practice tests are meant to help children develop critical thinking and test-taking skills. A "score" (a percentile rank) cannot be obtained from these. (See page 6 for more on gifted test scoring.)

3. Directions and Answer Keys for Practice Tests (p. 12, p. 92-94)

Please use a pair of scissors to cut out pages **92-94**. These pages provide answer keys for the practice tests. They also include the directions, as well as additional explanations for some of the questions . (To mimic actual tests, the directions are separate from the child's pages in the practice tests.)

4. Afterword (p. 95-96)

Information on additional books and your child's certificate

A NOTE ON FILLING IN "BUBBLES"

Your child may or may not have to fill in "bubbles" (the circles) to indicate answer choices. When taking a standardized gifted test, if your child is at the Pre-K level, (s)he will most likely only have to point to the answer choice. If your child is at the Kindergarten or First Grade level, (s)he may have to fill in bubbles. Check with your testing site regarding its "bubble" use. We have included "bubbles" in this publication to distinguish the answer choices.

If your child is at the Kindergarten or First Grade level, show him/her the "bubbles" under the answer choices. Show your child how to fill in the bubble to indicate his/her answer choice. If your child needs to change his/her answer, (s)he should erase the original mark and fill in the new choice.

A NOTE ON THE QUESTIONS

Because each child has different cognitive abilities, the questions in this book are at varied skill levels. The exercises may or may not require a great deal of parental guidance to complete, depending on your child's ability.

We suggest showing your child the example questions on pages 7-10 as a brief introduction before (s)he attempts to complete a practice test. Make sure there is not any confusion about what the questions are asking the child to do.

Unless your child is already familiar with NNAT2® / NNAT3® question format (through completion of other test prep materials or other gifted tests), we suggest completing the first practice test together.

WHAT YOU NEED

- This NNAT® TEST PREP book
- Pencil and eraser for your child
- Directions & Answer Keys (pages **92-94**) cut out and by your side

ABOUT THE NNAT2® / NNAT3®

Gifted tests, like the NNAT2® / NNAT3®, assess a child's cognitive abilities, reasoning skills, and problem-solving aptitude. NNAT® stands for Naglieri Nonverbal Ability Test®. As a "non-verbal" test, this test does not require test-takers to listen to multiple question prompts, nor does it assess verbal comprehension or verbal skills. Testing procedures vary by school and/or program. These tests may be given individually or in a small group environment, by a teacher or other testing examiner. These tests may be used as the single determinant for admission to a selective school or to a school's gifted program. However, some schools/programs use these tests in combination with individual IQ tests adminis-tered by psychologists or as part of a student "portfolio." Other schools use them together with tests like Iowa Assessments™ to measure academic achievement. See the next page for more information on test sections. **Check with your testing site to determine its specific testing procedures.**

Here is a general summary of the scoring process for multiple-choice standardized gifted tests. **Please check with your school/program for its specific scoring and admissions requirements.** First, your child's raw score is established. The raw score equals the number of questions your daughter/son correctly answered. Points are not deducted for questions answered incorrectly. Next, this score is compared to other test-takers of his/her same age group using various indices to then calculate your child's percentile rank. If your child achieved the percentile rank of 98%, then (s)he scored as well as or better than 98% of test-takers in his/her age group. In general, most gifted programs only accept top performers of *at least* 98% or *higher*. Please note that a percentile rank "score" cannot be obtained from our practice material. This material has not been given to a large enough sample of test-takers to develop any kind of base score necessary for accurate percentile rank calculations.

NNAT2® AND NNAT3®
- The design of these two tests is **very** similar.
- Both consist of 48 questions and last approximately 30 minutes.
- Both have the same two question types in Level A and the same three question types in Level B (see p. 7).
- Both tests' questions consist of shapes, lines, and figures.
- In the NNAT2®, test questions' colors could be blue, yellow, white and black.
- In the NNAT3®, test questions' colors could be blue, yellow, white, black and green.

NNAT® LEVEL A AND NNAT® LEVEL B
- Level A is for Kindergarten. Level B is for First Grade.
- Both last approximately 30 minutes with 48 questions consisting of shapes, lines, and figures.

- Level A has two question types: Pattern Completion and Reasoning by Analogy.
- Level B has three question types: Pattern Completion, Reasoning by Analogy, and Serial Reasoning.

NNAT2® / NNAT3® QUESTION TYPES & EXAMPLES

The book's three Practice Tests are organized by question type. Below are brief explanations and examples of the three question types.

QUESTION TYPE 1: PATTERN COMPLETION

Here, your child selects the answer to go in place of the question mark to complete the "puzzle."

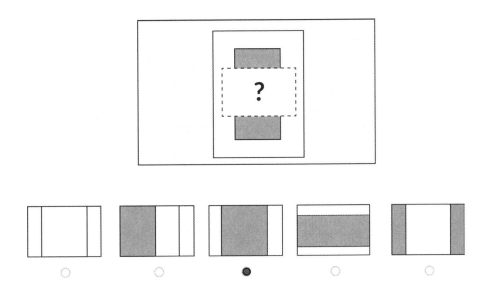

Your child should look closely at the pattern's elements: lines, colors, shapes, and any other figures.

Then, (s)he should do the same with the area around the white box. How do the elements look next to the white box with the question mark? Examine things like color, length, width and quantity.

Ask your child what (s)he thinks the "puzzle" would look like below the white box, if (s)he could pick it up.

Sample Directions: Here is a puzzle where a piece is missing. (Point to the box that has the question mark.) Which one of the answer choices (point to the row of answer choices) would go here? (Point to the box that has the question mark again.)

Be sure that your child looks at the overall picture (or pattern). Some questions will require your child to look beyond the area touching the white box and at the pattern presented in the overall picture as well. See the example on the next page involving the pattern of blue triangles and their sizes.

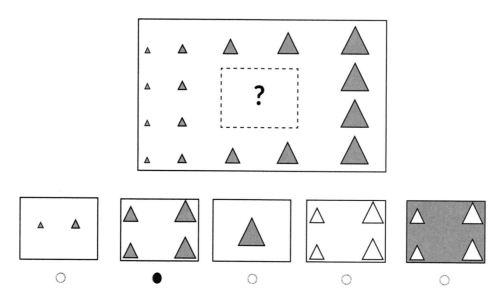

Sample Directions: Here is a puzzle where a piece is missing. (Point to the box that has the question mark.) Which one of the answer choices (point to the row of answer choices) would go here? (Point to the box that has the question mark again.)

QUESTION TYPE 2: REASONING BY ANALOGY

Here, your child selects the answer to go in place of the question mark to complete the analogy. Questions contain geometric figures. Your child will determine how the figures change across the rows.

To help your child understand Reasoning By Analogy questions, this wording may be helpful:
"(Point to the top left box.) This changes to this. (Point to the top right box.) Then, (point to the bottom left box) this would change to (point to the box with the question mark) ___. We need to figure out what would go here."
You could also use wording that is common for all analogy questions (not only in NNAT® analogies).
"(Point to the top left box.) This is to that. (Point to the top right box.) As this (point to the bottom left box) is to (point to the box with the question mark) ___. We need to figure out what would go here."

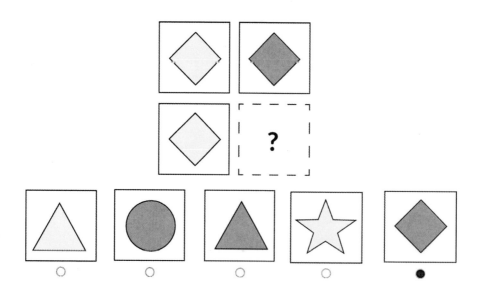

Simple Reasoning By Analogy questions contain one "change," while more challenging questions contain more than one "change." For example, the previous question had one "change" (color). Here are <u>simple</u> examples with one change:

Size Change

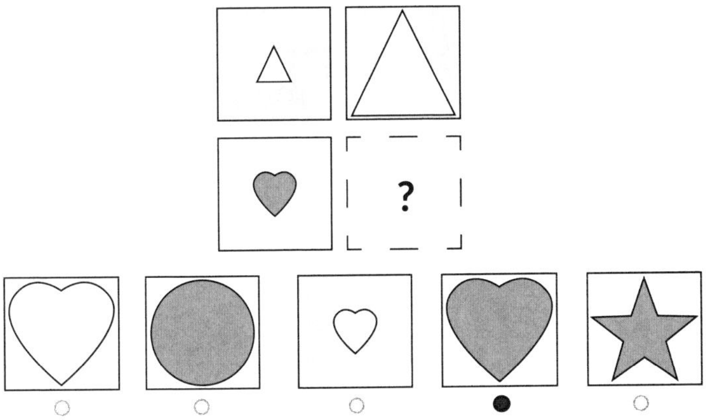

Shape Change

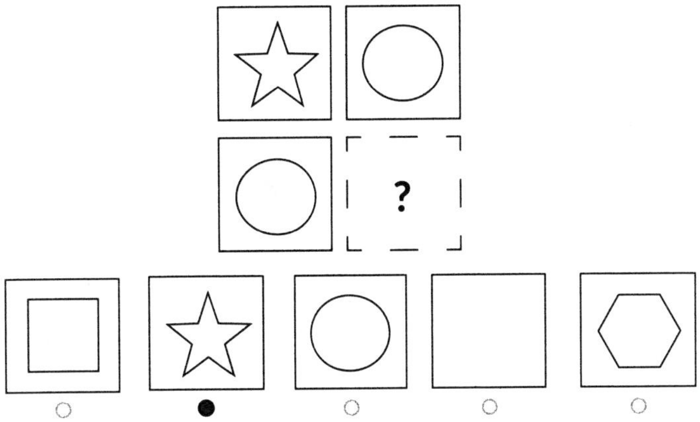

Color Change/ Color Reversal:

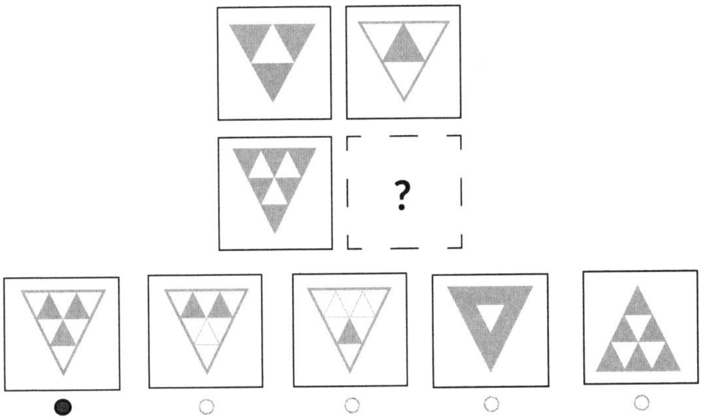

Adding/ Removing Figures (here, 1 is added)

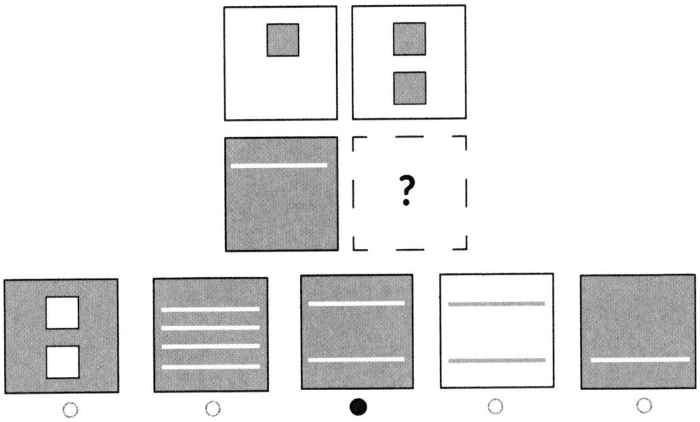

Same (No Change)

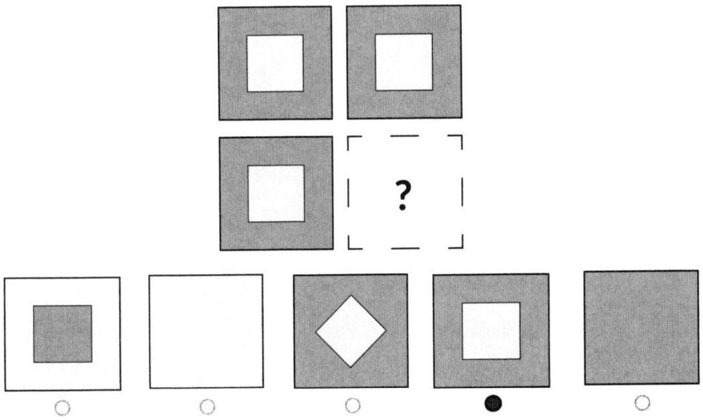

Whole to Part (or, Part to Whole in other questions)

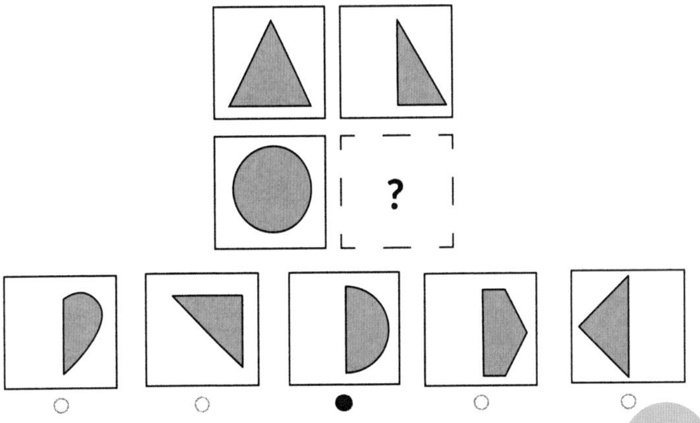

Rotation*

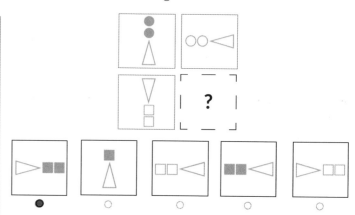

Rotation <u>and</u> Color Change*

*In the questions, note the *type* of rotation: clockwise, counter-clockwise, and to what degree (i.e., 180 vs. 90).

*This question has <u>two</u> "changes" and is more representative of a Level B question.

QUESTION TYPE 3: SERIAL REASONING

Serial Reasoning questions have similar elements and require similar problem solving skills as Reasoning By Analogy. However, they are arranged on a 3 x 3 (9-box) matrix. To find the answer, your child must closely examine how the elements in each box change across the rows and down the columns. Serial Reasoning only appears in Level B. If your child will take Level A, in the Practice Tests, complete these as "challenge questions" while working together.

It is important that your child does not rush through these. The answers can be easily missed at first.
1- Have your child look carefully at the top row. Can (s)he find a pattern?
2- Have your child look carefully at the middle row. Can (s)he find a pattern similar to the one found in the top row?
3- Have your child look carefully at the bottom row. What would go in the empty box to complete the pattern?
If (s)he does not find a pattern across the rows, then (s)he should try to find a pattern down the columns.
1- Have your child look carefully at the first column. Can (s)he find a pattern?
2- Have your child look carefully at the second column. Can (s)he find a pattern similar to the first column?
3- Have your child look carefully at the last column. What would go in the empty box to complete the pattern?
(Each row/column has either a heart, star or trapezoid and has one shape filled with either dots, vertical lines or is plain.)

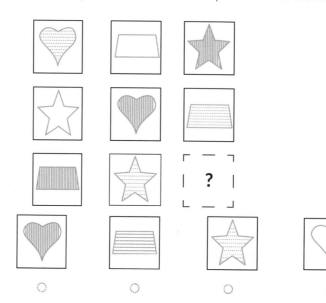

TEST-TAKING TIPS

WORK THROUGH THE EXERCISE: We suggest completing the first practice test together (unless your child is already familiar with the NNAT® question format through completion of other test prep materials or other gifted tests). Go through the exercises together by talking about them: what the exercise is asking the child to do and what makes the answer choices correct/incorrect. This will not only familiarize your child with working through exercises, it will also help him/her develop a process of elimination (getting rid of any answer choices that are incorrect).

ANSWER CHOICES: Make sure your child looks at **each** answer choice. You may wish to point to each answer choice if you notice your child not looking at each one.

GUESSING: For the test outlined in this book, test-takers receive points for the number of correct answers. It is advantageous to at least guess instead of leaving a question unanswered. If your child says that (s)he does not know the answer, (s)he should first eliminate any answers that are obviously not correct. Then, (s)he can guess from those remaining.

CHOOSE ONE ANSWER: Remind your child to choose only ONE answer. If your child has a test with "answer bubbles," remind him/her that he/she must fill in only ONE bubble per question. If your child must instead point to an answer, remind him/her to point to only one answer per question.

COMMON SENSE TIPS: Children are like adults when it comes to common sense exam-readiness for test day. Make sure your child:

- is familiar with the test site (If the exam will be at a location that is new to your child, go to the testing site together before test day. Simply driving by or walking by the outside of the building not only ensures you know how to reach the site; it also will give your child a sense of familiarity, come test day.)
- is well-rested
- has eaten a breakfast for sustained energy and concentration (complex carbohydrates and protein; avoid foods/drinks high in sugar)
- has a chance to use the restroom prior to the test (The administrator may not allow a break during the test.)

Try not to get overly-stressed about the gifted testing process (as difficult as that may be). It is surprising how much children can sense from adults, and children learn best through play. So, the more fun that you can make test prep (by using something like a detective theme), the better.

PRACTICE TEST NOTES -

PRACTICE TEST COMPOSITION

- This book consists of three practice tests, with 50 questions each.
- Each of the three tests contains the three NNAT® question types:
- Pattern Completion (30 questions); #1 - #30 in each test
  P. 14-28 of Practice Test 1; P. 40-54 of Practice Test 2; P. 66-80 of Practice Test 3
- Reasoning By Analogy (14 questions); #31 - #44 in each test
  P. 29-35 of Practice Test 1; P. 55-61 of Practice Test 2; P. 81-87 of Practice Test 3
- Serial Reasoning (6 questions); #45 - #50 in each test
  P. 36-38 of Practice Test 1; P. 62-64 of Practice Test 2; P. 88-90 of Practice Test 3

QUESTION TYPE COMPOSITION

- The first few questions in each section (Pattern Completion, Reasoning By Analogy, Serial Reasoning) of each practice test begin with relatively simple questions.
- The first few Pattern Completion questions in Practice Test 1 and Practice Test 2 are fairly simple, compared to the latter questions in Practice Test 1 and Practice Test 2, as well as Practice Test 3.
- In Practice Test 3, the first few Pattern Completion questions are a bit more difficult than in the Practice Test 1 and Practice Test 2.
- The same is true with the Reasoning By Analogy questions.
- This is NOT true with the Serial Reasoning questions. As explained before, Serial Reasoning questions only appear in Level B (First Grade). If your child will take the Level A exam and/or is in Kindergarten, you should complete these together with your child as "challenge questions."

DIRECTIONS & ANSWER KEYS

- Please cut out p. **92-94** (the Directions & Answer Keys) for the three tests.
- Please be sure to read the instructions on p. 92.

ADDITIONAL PRACTICE -

WWW.GATEWAYGIFTED.COM

- We offer another NNAT® Level A book, available at www.GatewayGifted.com and Amazon.com®.
- We offer a FREE e-book with 40+ gifted test prep questions, go to: www.GatewayGifted.com for yours.

THE SHAPE DETECTIVES *(Read this page with your child.)*

Alex

May

Sophie

Freddie

Max

Anya

We're the Shape Detectives. We need another member to join our detective agency. We think YOU have what it takes!

"What does a detective do?" you may ask. Well, a detective figures out puzzles, solves problems, and finds answers to questions.

To prove you're ready to join us, you'll put your skills to the test in this book. Together with your mom, dad or other adult, you need to solve puzzles. The adult helping you will explain what to do, so listen carefully!

A good detective:
- Pays attention and listens closely
- Looks carefully at all choices before answering a question
- Keeps trying even if some questions are hard

Your parent (or other adult) will tell you which questions to do. After finishing them all, you will become a Shape Detective! (Remember, it's more important to answer the questions the right way than to try to finish them really fast.) After you're done, you'll get your very own detective certificate.

When you're ready to start the puzzles, write your name here: _____

PRACTICE TEST 1 BEGINS ON THE NEXT PAGE

1

○   ○   ○   ○   ○

2

○   ○   ○   ○   ○

3

4

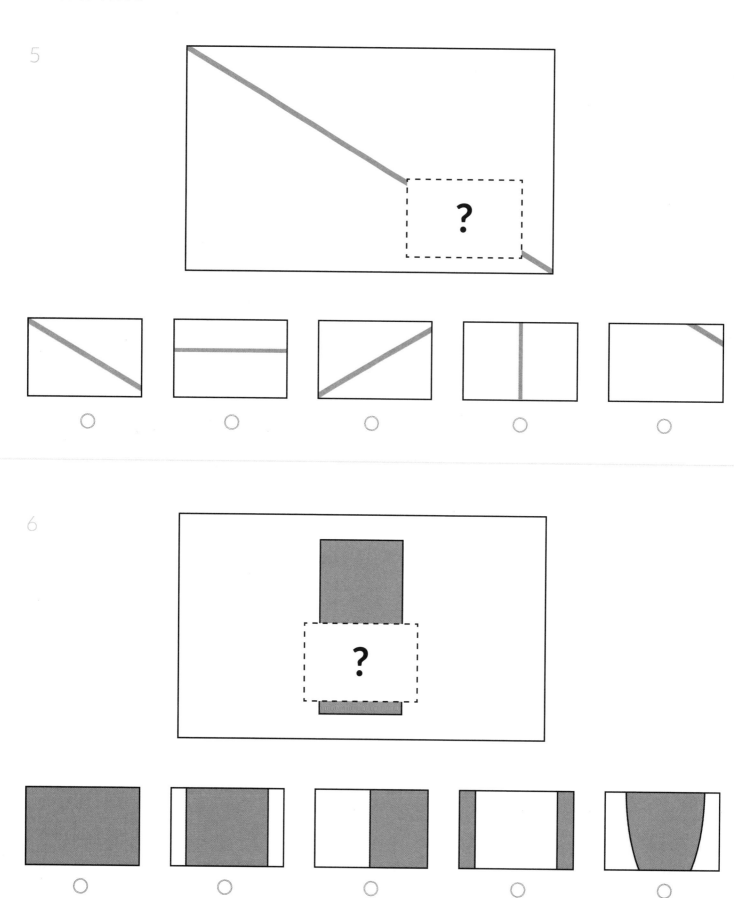

5

6

7

8

9

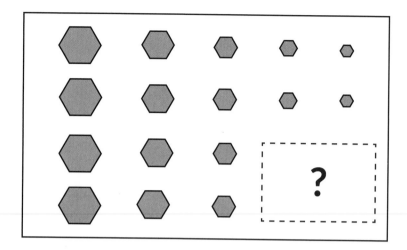

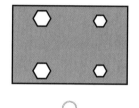  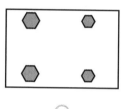 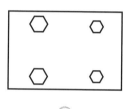 

○ ○ ○ ○ ○

10

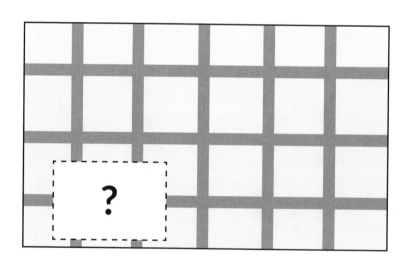

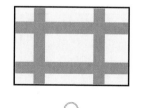 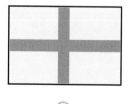   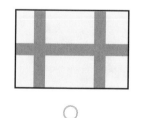

○ ○ ○ ○ ○

11

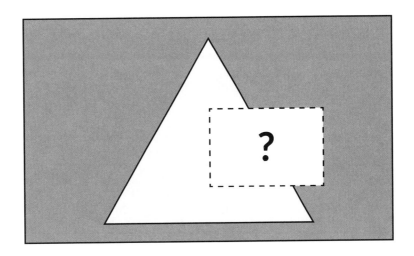

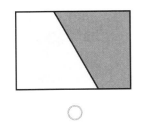 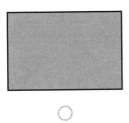 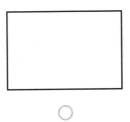 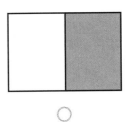 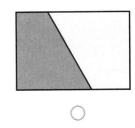

○   ○   ○   ○   ○

12

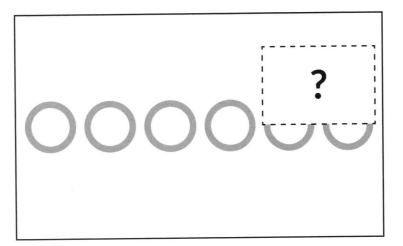

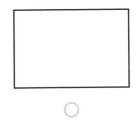 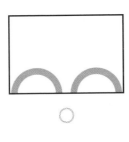 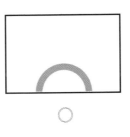 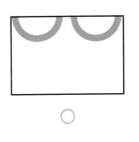 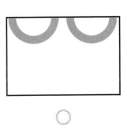

○   ○   ○   ○   ○

13

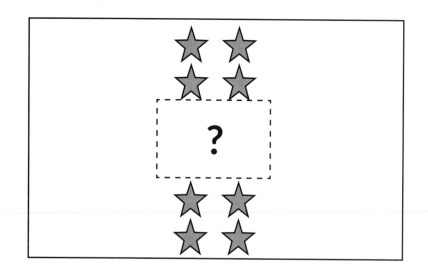

○ ○ ○ ○ ○

14

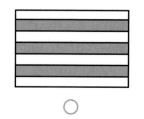 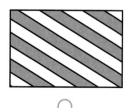 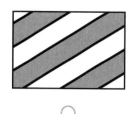 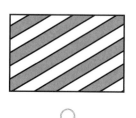 

○ ○ ○ ○ ○

15

16

17

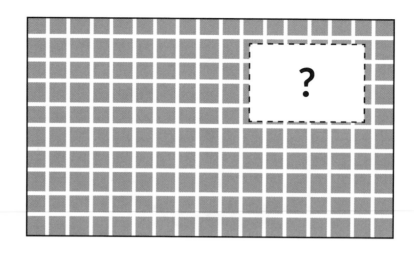

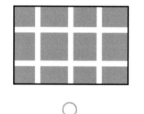 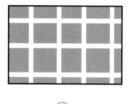 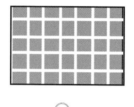 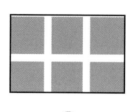 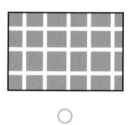

○   ○   ○   ○   ○

18

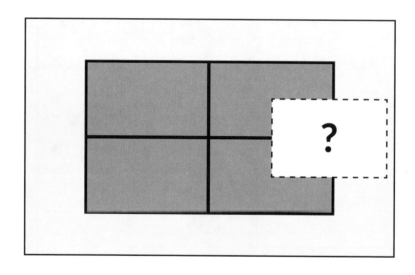

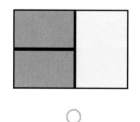 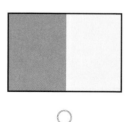 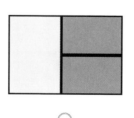 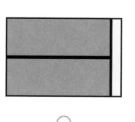 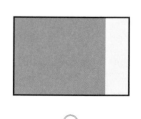

○   ○   ○   ○   ○

19

20

21

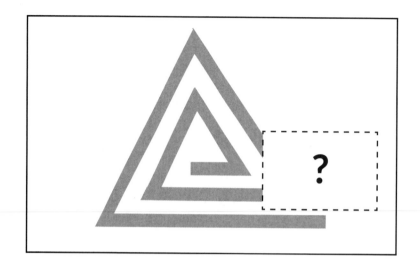

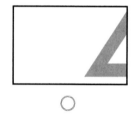 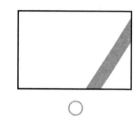 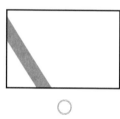  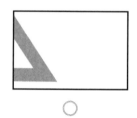

○ ○ ○ ○ ○

22

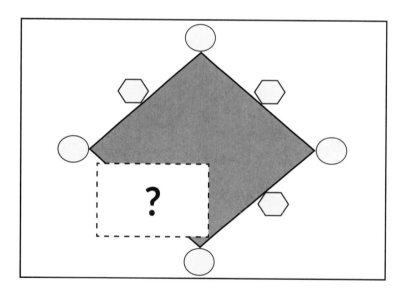

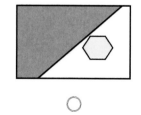 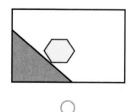 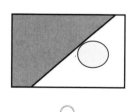 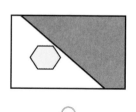 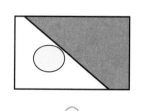

○ ○ ○ ○ ○

23

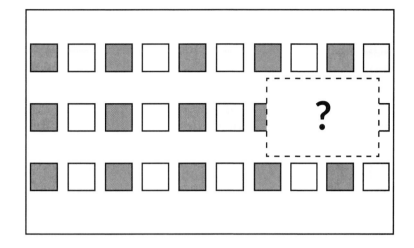

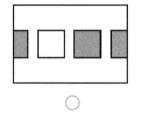

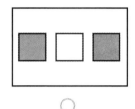

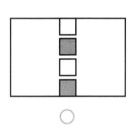

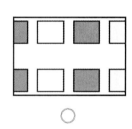

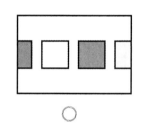

○   ○   ○   ○   ○

24

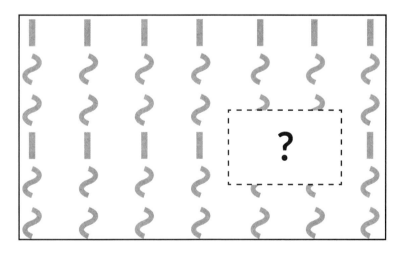

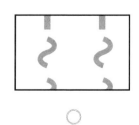

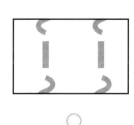

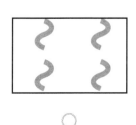

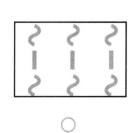

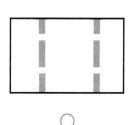

○   ○   ○   ○   ○

25

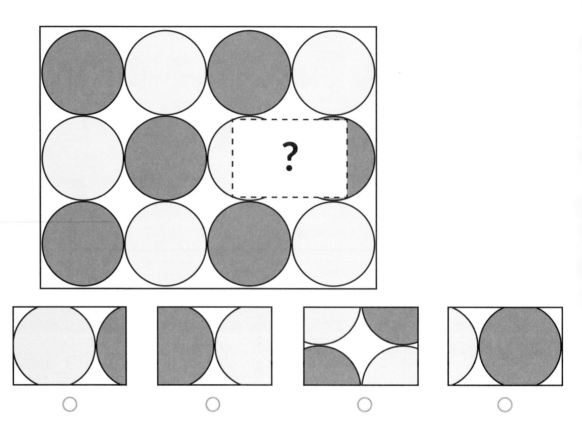

26

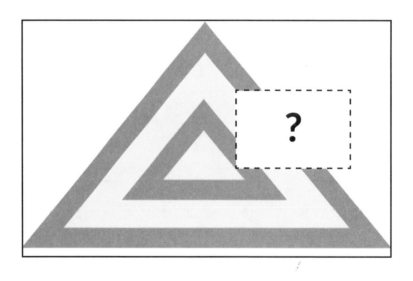

27

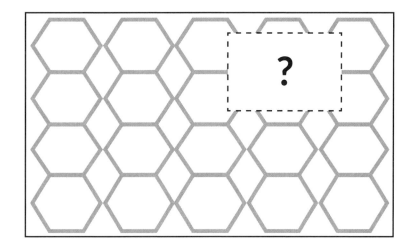

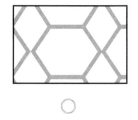   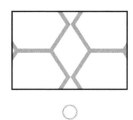   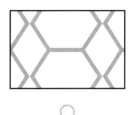   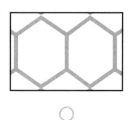   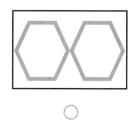

○   ○   ○   ○   ○

28

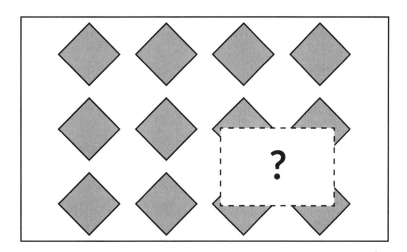

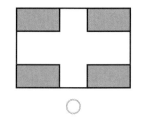   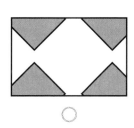   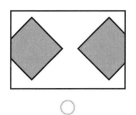   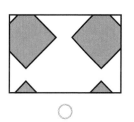   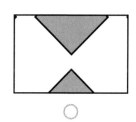

○   ○   ○   ○   ○

29

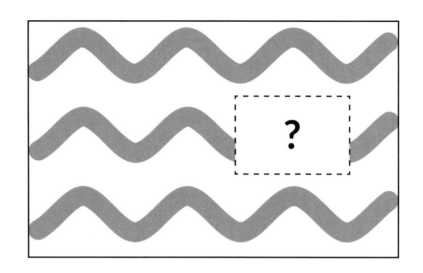

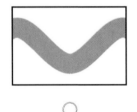   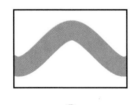   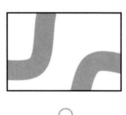   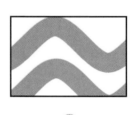   

○   ○   ○   ○   ○

30

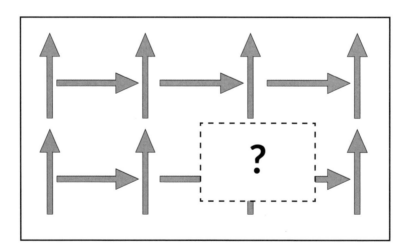

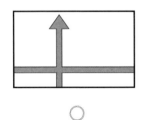   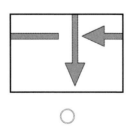   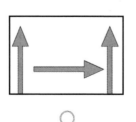   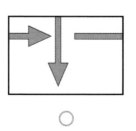   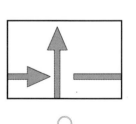

○   ○   ○   ○   ○

31

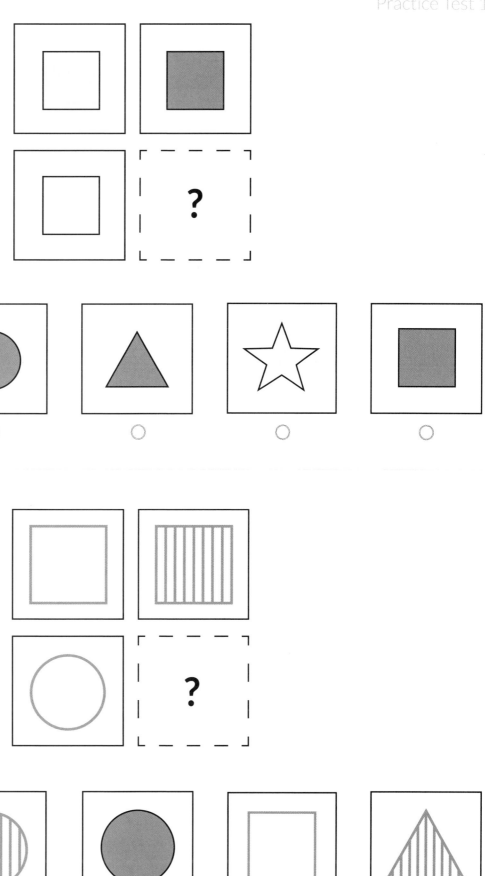

32

33

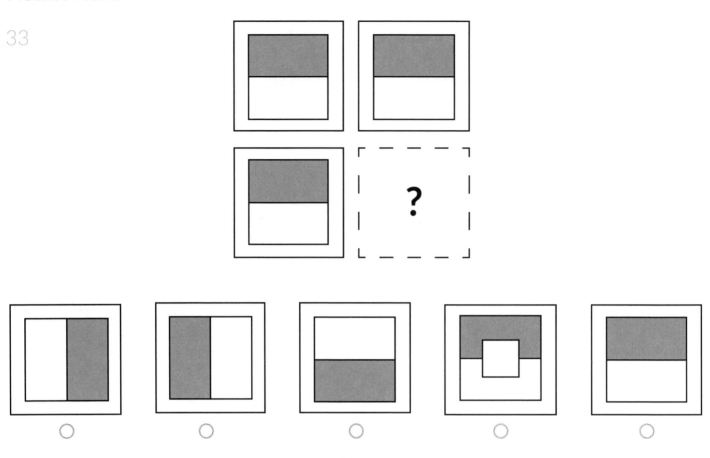

34

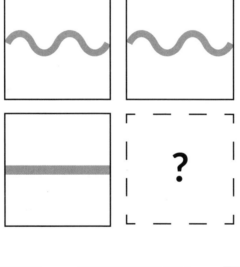

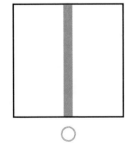 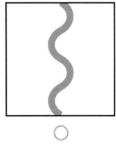 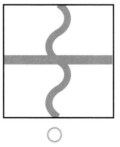  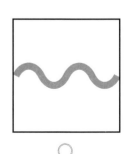

35

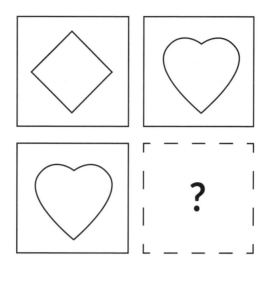

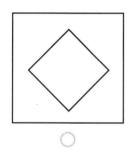    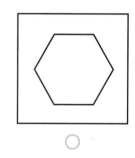

○   ○   ○   ○   ○

36

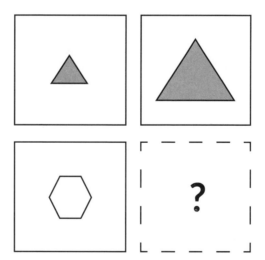

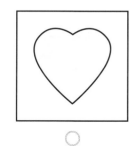 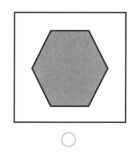 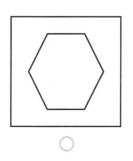 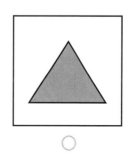 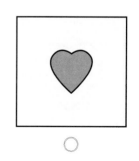

○   ○   ○   ○   ○

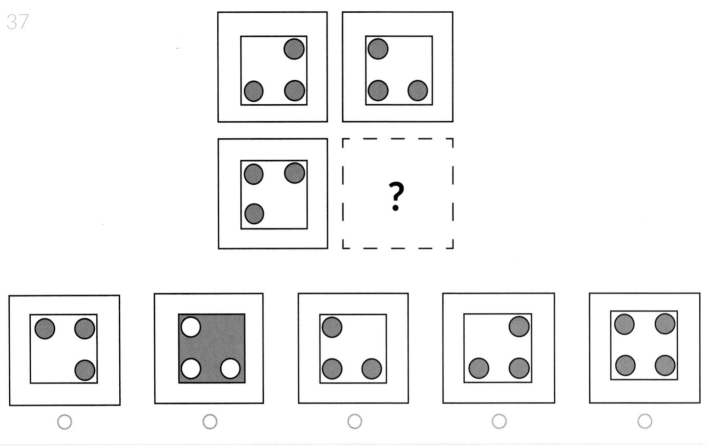

38

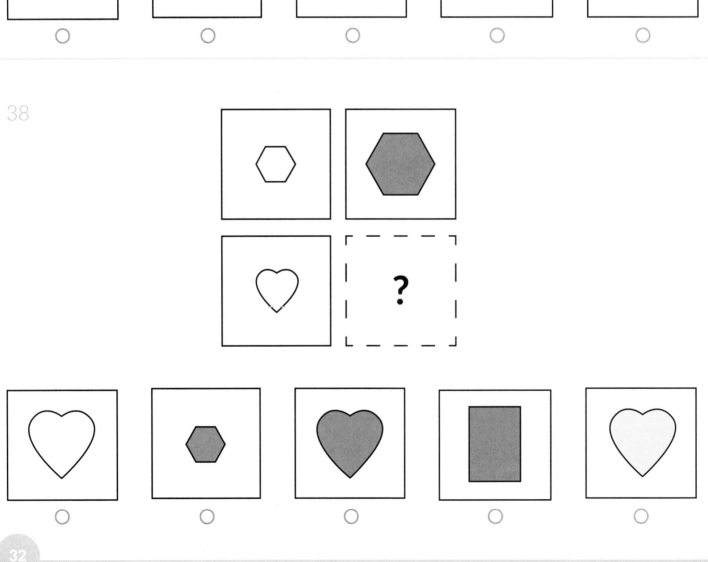

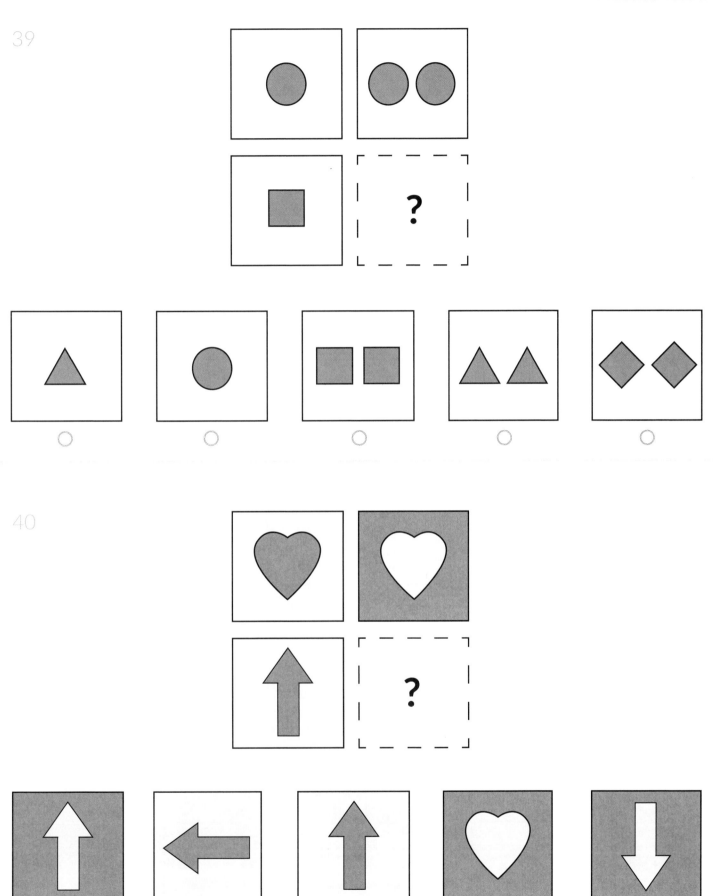

41

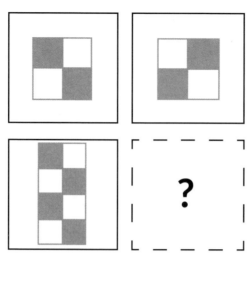

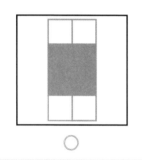

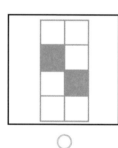
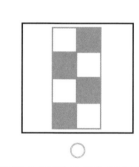

○　　　　○　　　　○　　　　○　　　　○

42

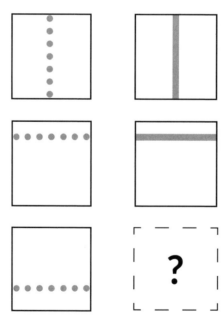

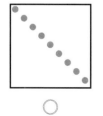

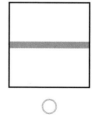

○　　　　○　　　　○　　　　○　　　　○

43

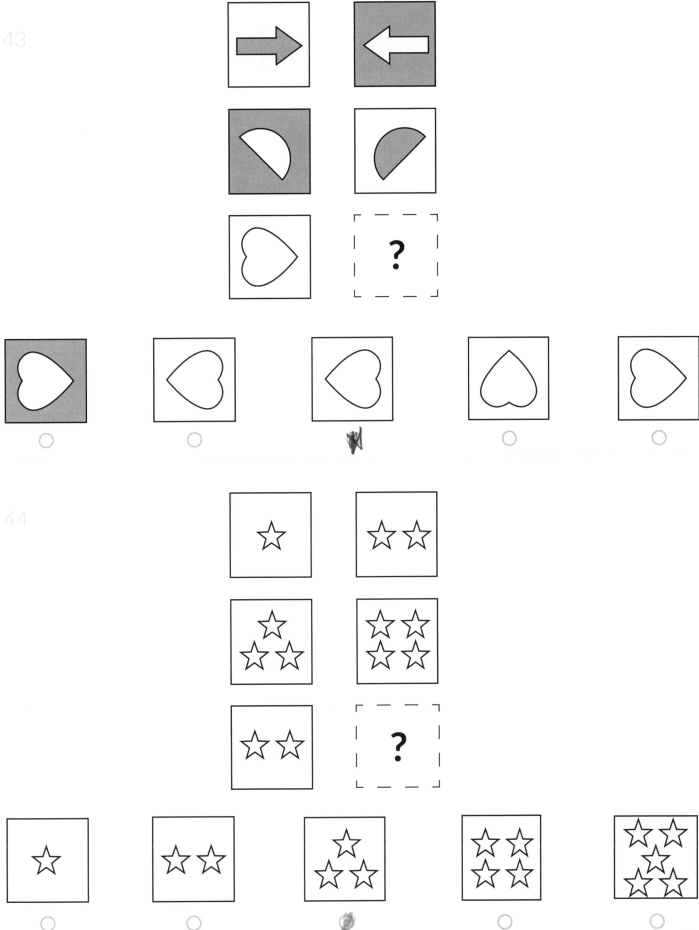

44

45

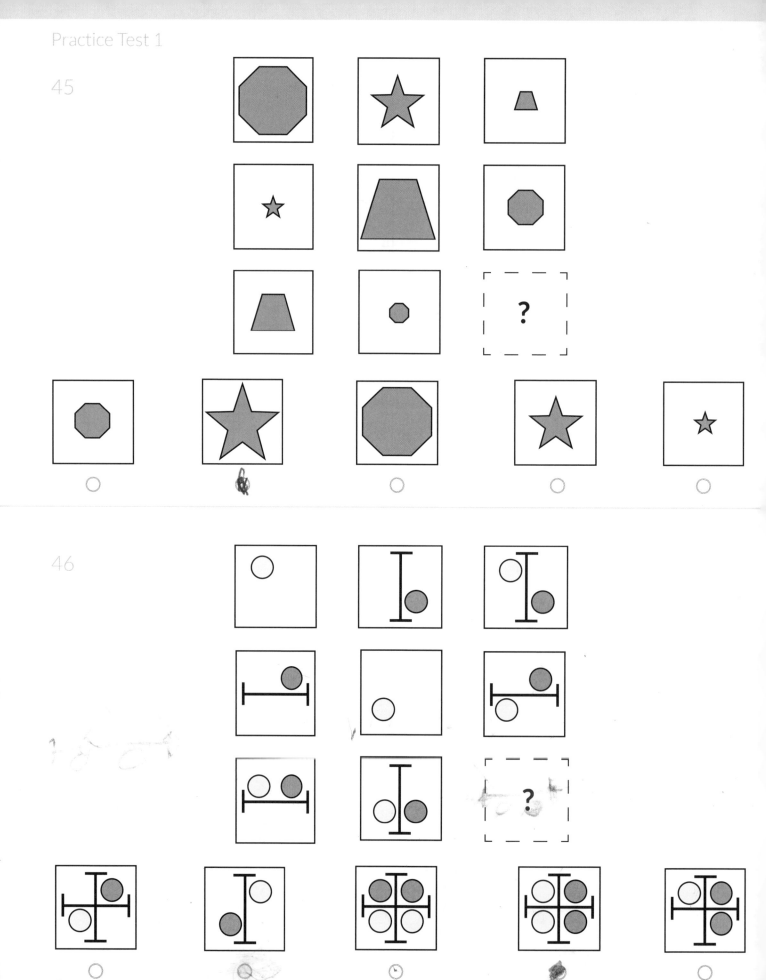

46

47

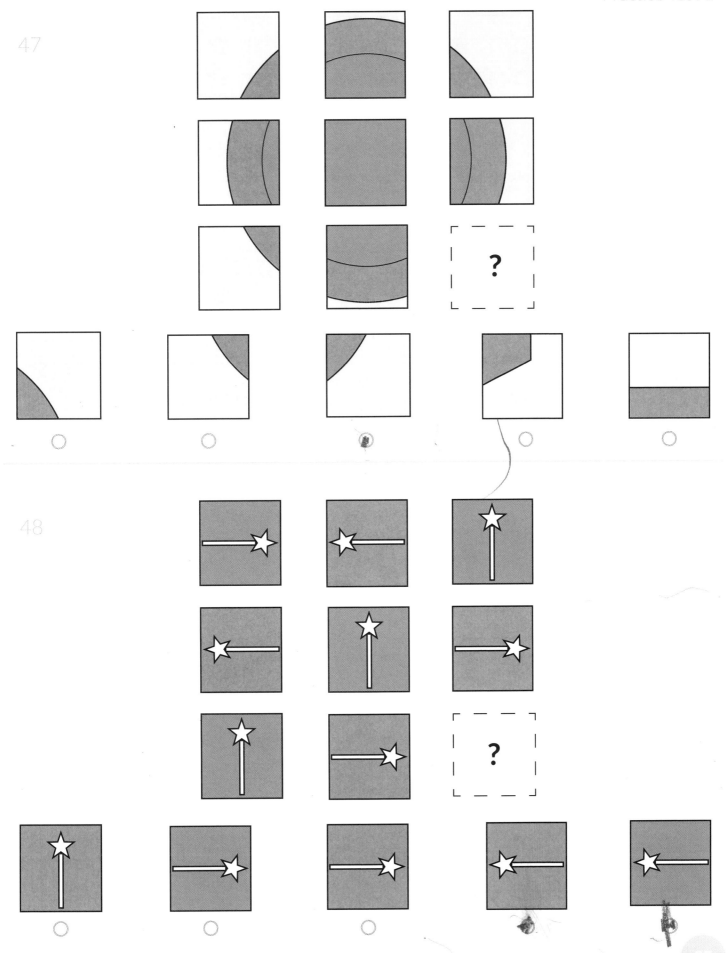

48

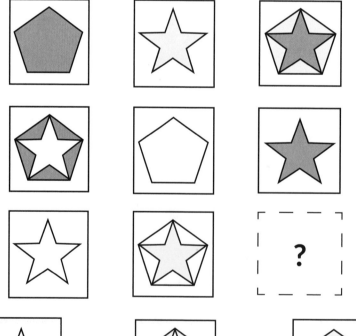

50

- End of Practice Test 1 -
- Practice Test 2 begins on the next page -

1

2

3

○   ○   ○   ○   ○

4

○   ○   ○   ○   ○

5

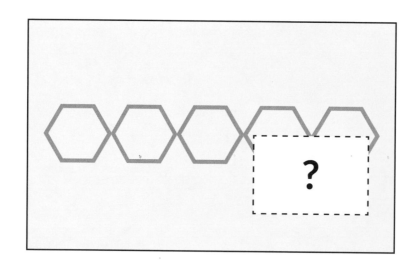

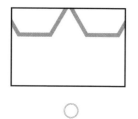      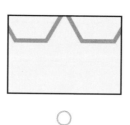      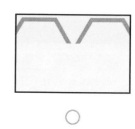

○   ○   ○   ○   ○

6

   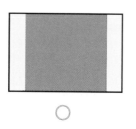      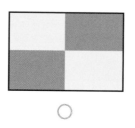   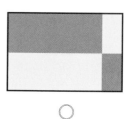

○   ○   ○   ○   ○

7

8

9

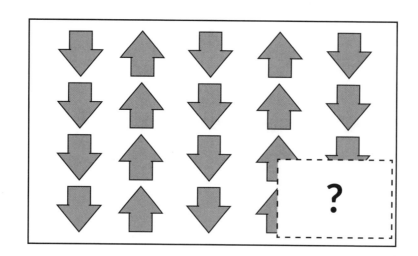

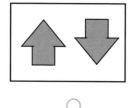 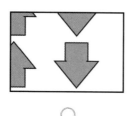 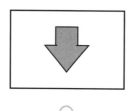 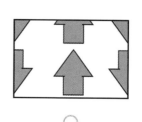 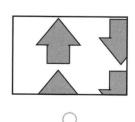

○ ○ ○ ○ ○

10

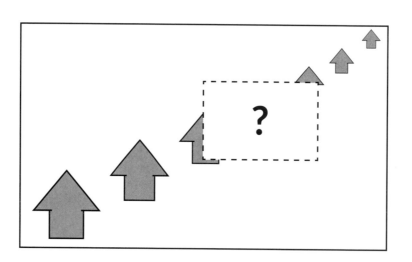

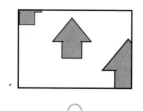 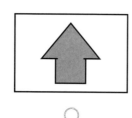 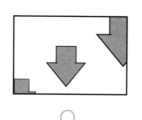 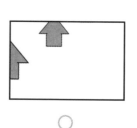 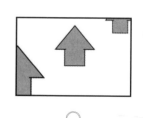

○ ○ ○ ○ ○

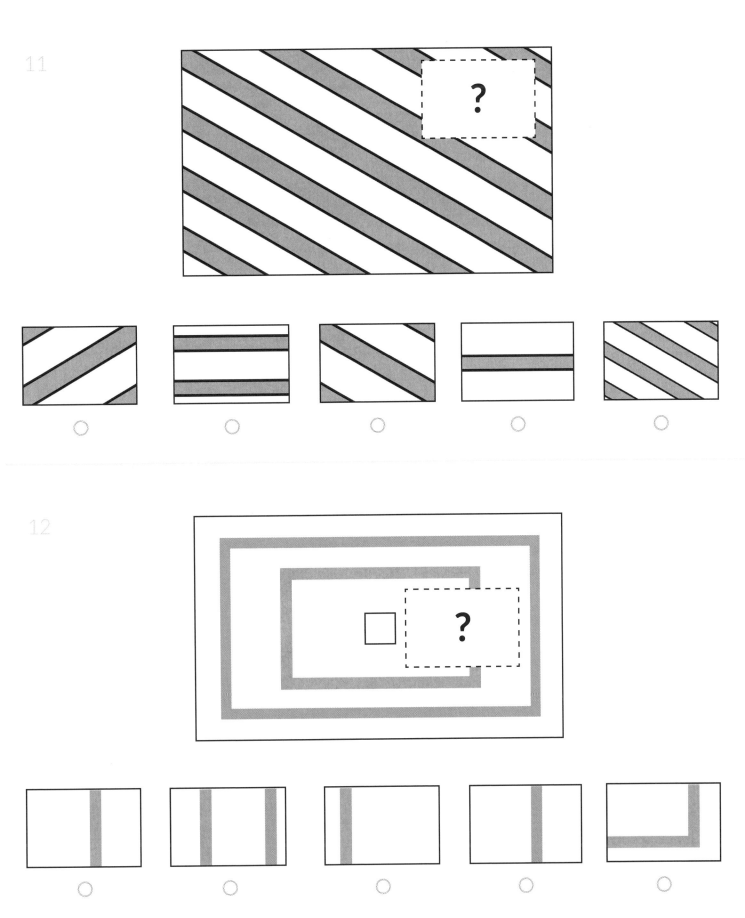

11

12

13

14

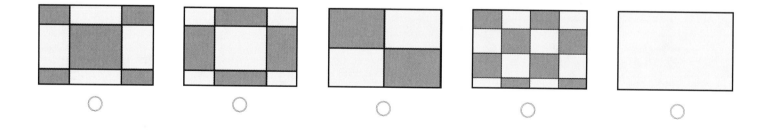

15

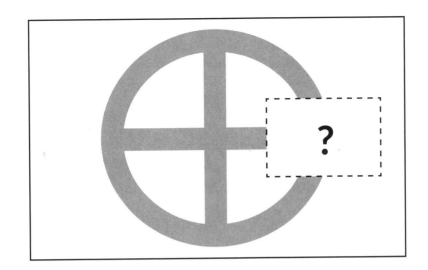

16

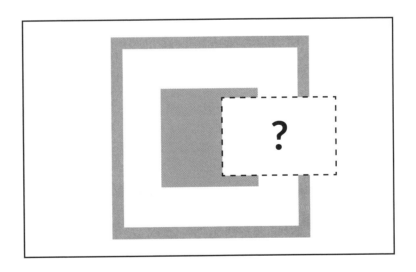

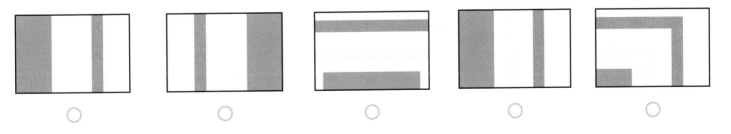

17

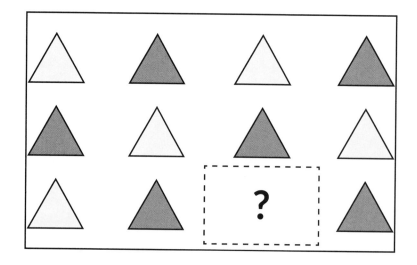

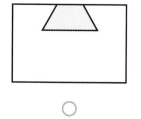 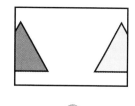 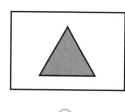 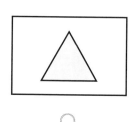 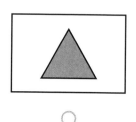

○ ○ ○ ○ ○

18

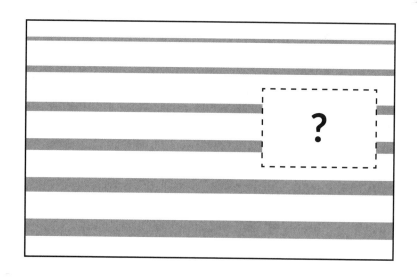

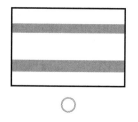 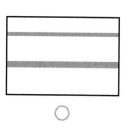 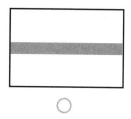 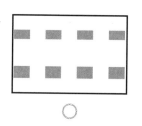 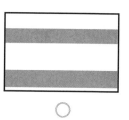

○ ○ ○ ○ ○

19

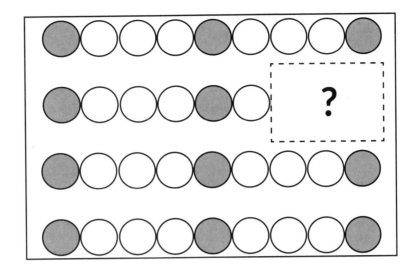

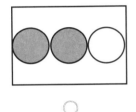

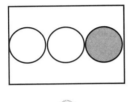

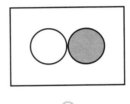

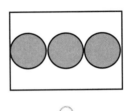

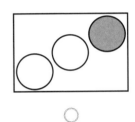

20

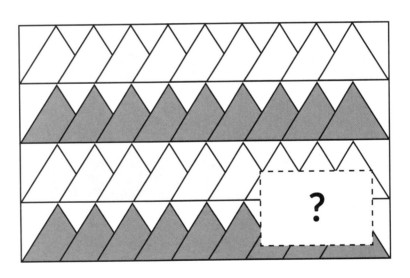

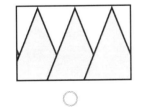

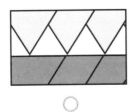

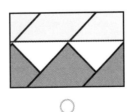

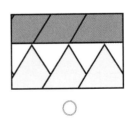

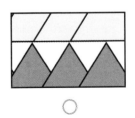

21

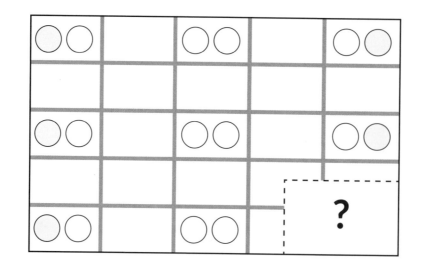

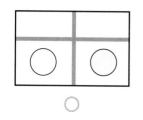   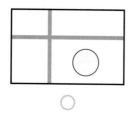   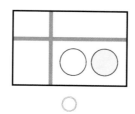   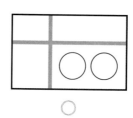   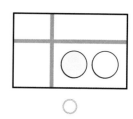

○   ○   ○   ○   ○

22

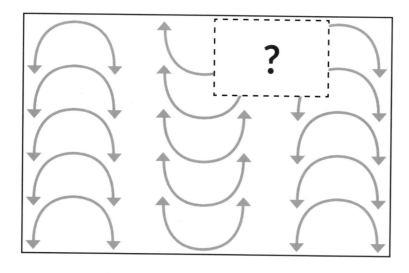

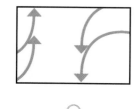   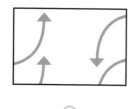   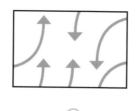   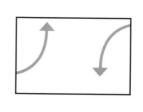   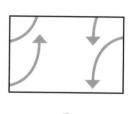

○   ○   ○   ○   ○

23

25

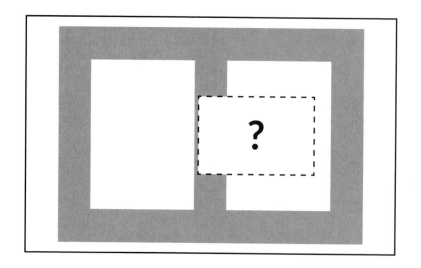

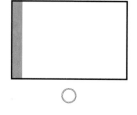 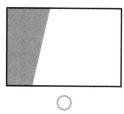 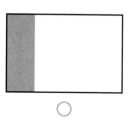 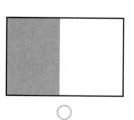 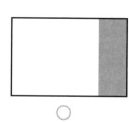

○   ○   ○   ○   ○

26

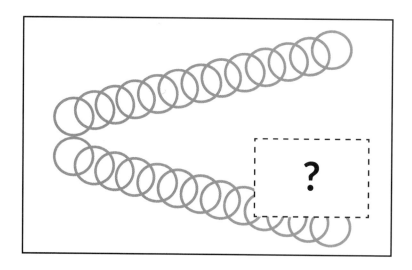

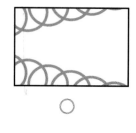 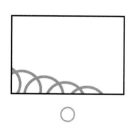 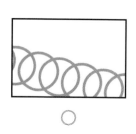 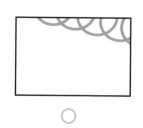 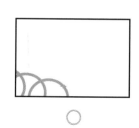

○   ○   ○   ○   ○

27

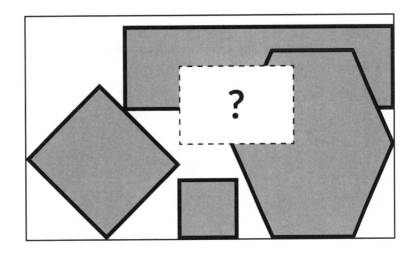

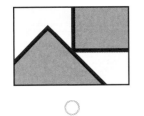 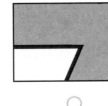 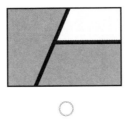  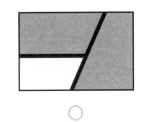

○ ○ ○ ○ ○

28

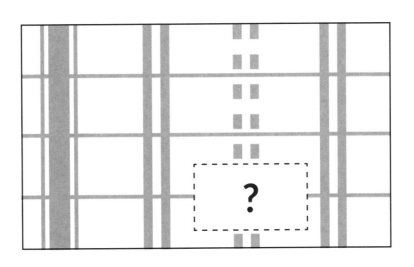

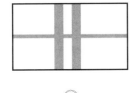 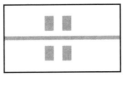 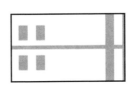 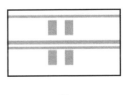 

○ ○ ○ ○ ○

29

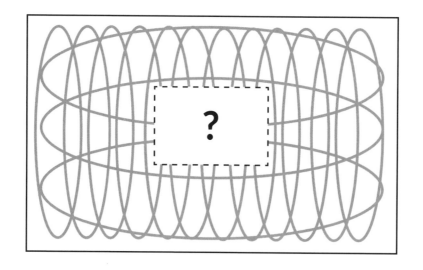

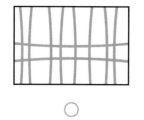 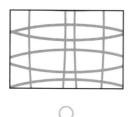 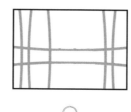 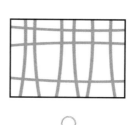 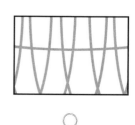

○ ○ ○ ○ ○

30

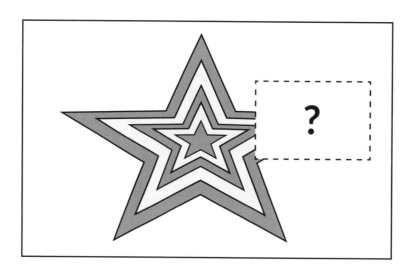

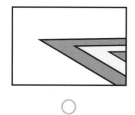 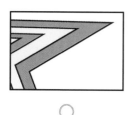  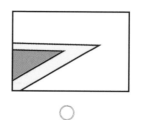 

○ ○ ○ ○ ○

31

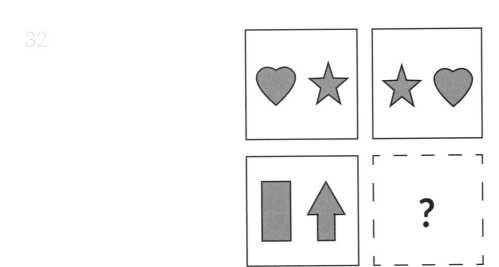

32

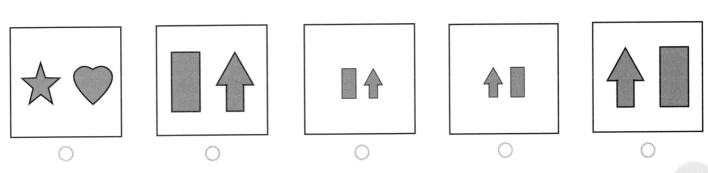

33

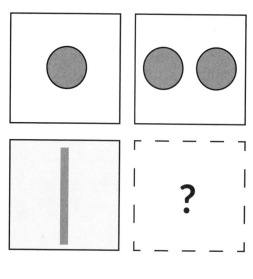

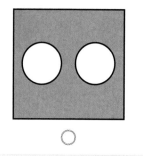

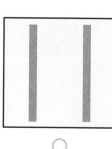

○ ○ ○ ○ ○

34

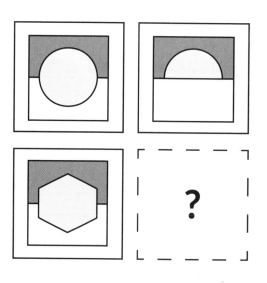

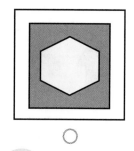
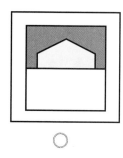
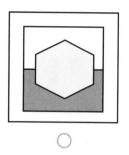
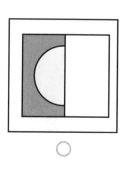
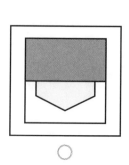

○ ○ ○ ○ ○

35

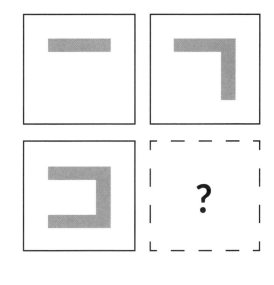

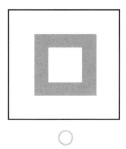

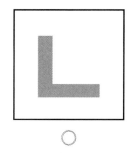

○ ○ ○ ○ ○

36

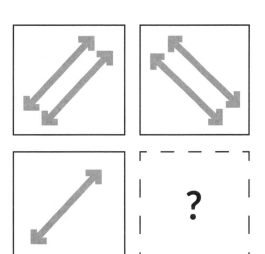

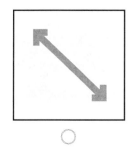

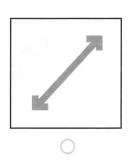

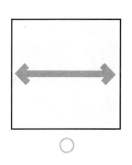

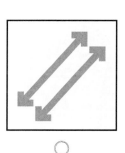

○ ○ ○ ○ ○

37

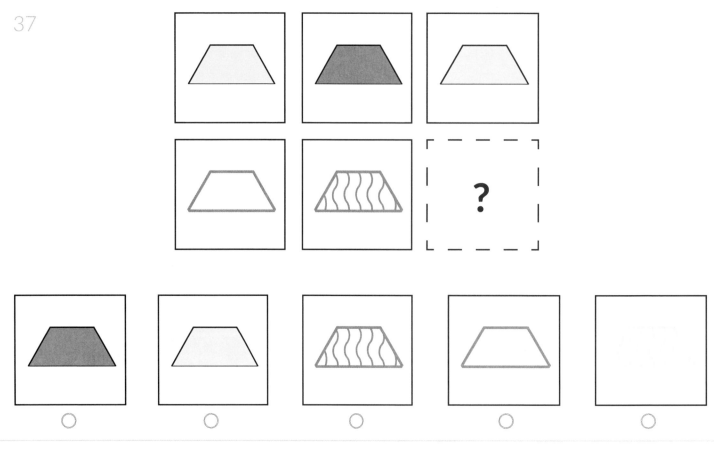

  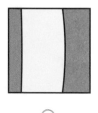  

○   ○   ○   ○   ○

38

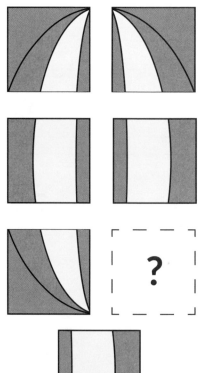

39

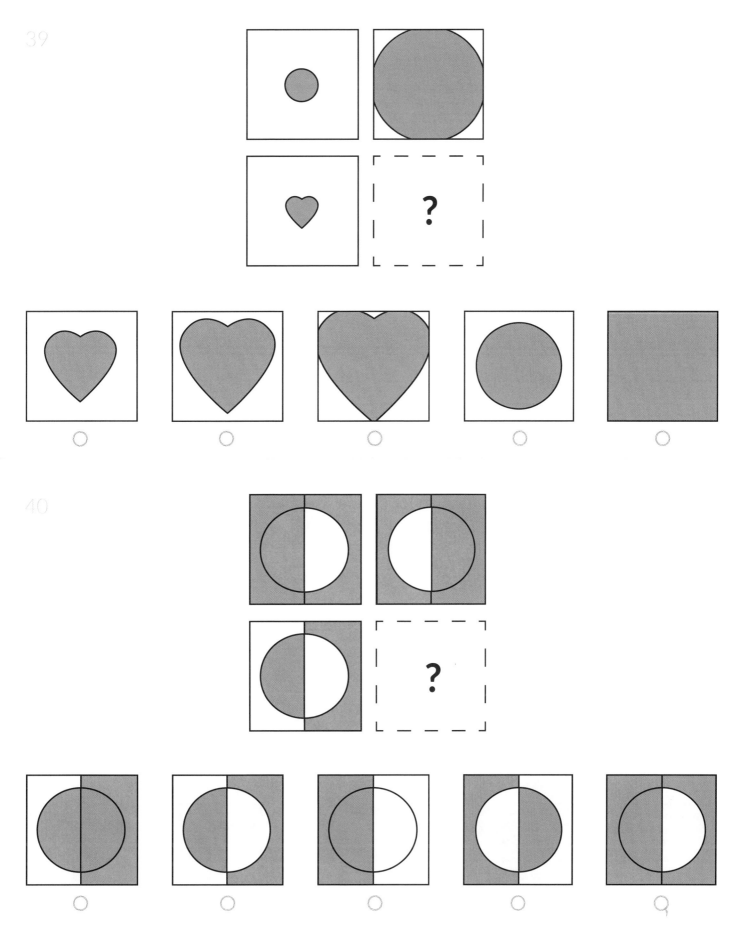

40

41

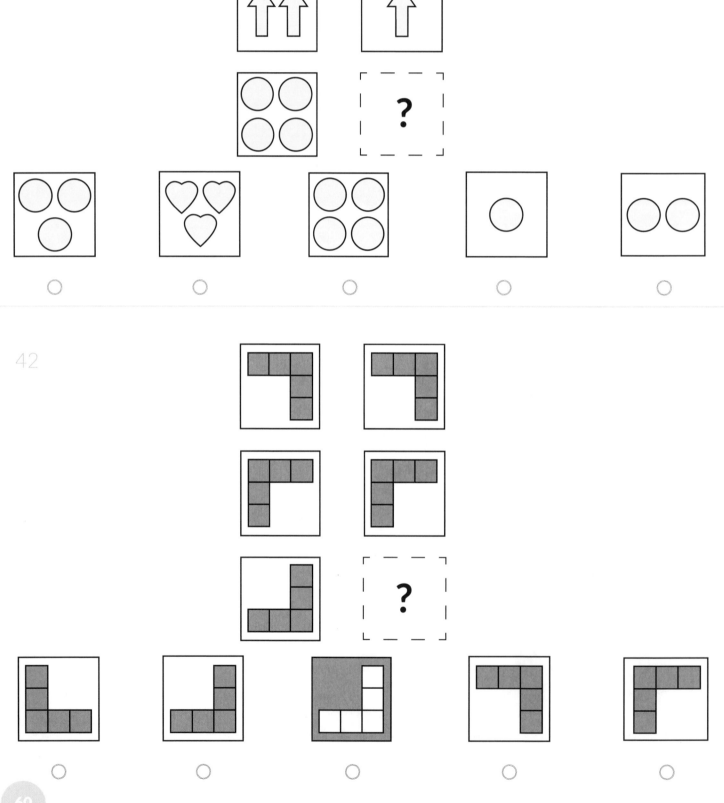

42

43

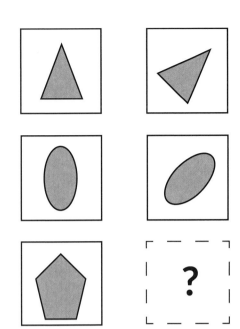

 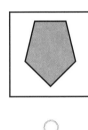  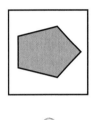 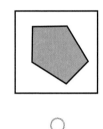

○ ○ ○ ○ ○

44

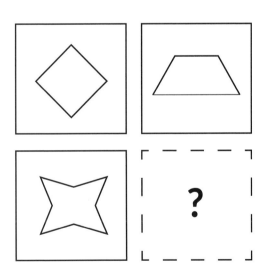

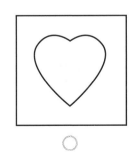 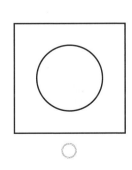 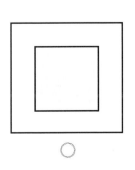 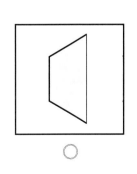 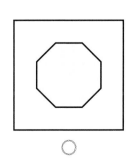

○ ○ ○ ○ ○

45

46

47

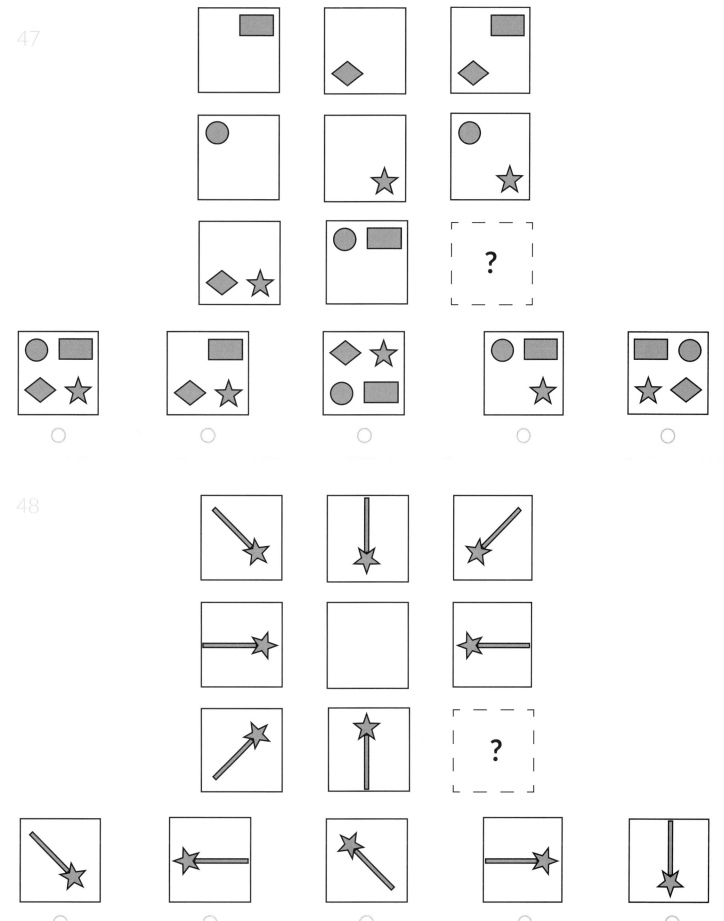

48

49

50

- End of Practice Test 2 -
- Practice Test 3 begins on the next page -

1

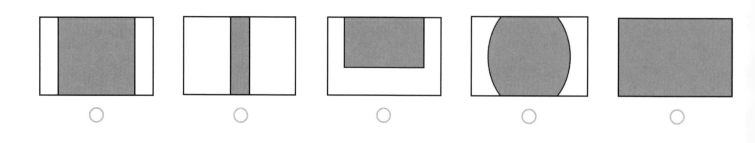

2

3

4

5

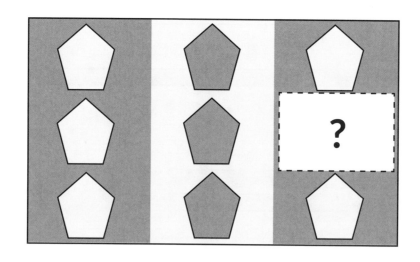

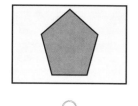   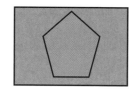   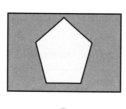   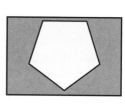   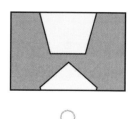

○   ○   ○   ○   ○

6

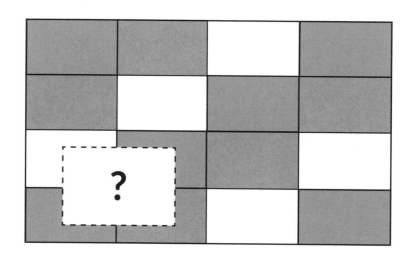

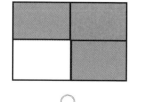   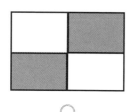   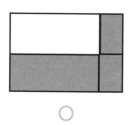   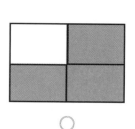   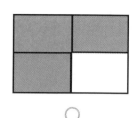

○   ○   ○   ○   ○

7

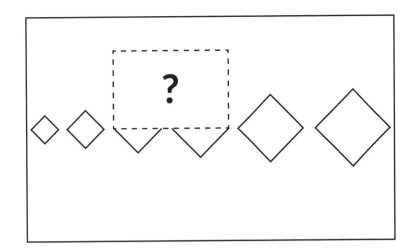

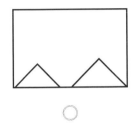 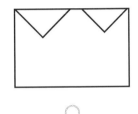 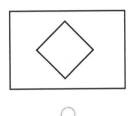 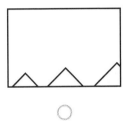 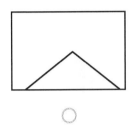

○ ○ ○ ○ ○

8

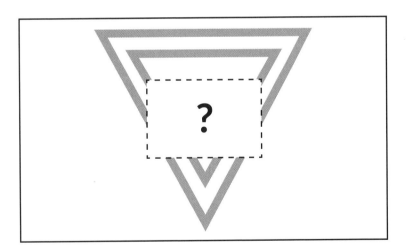

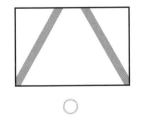 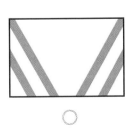 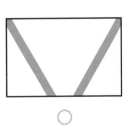 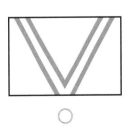 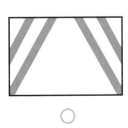

○ ○ ○ ○ ○

69

9

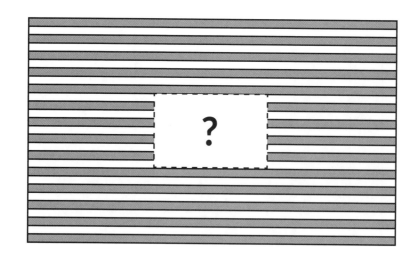

   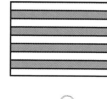      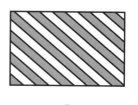   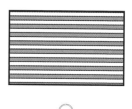

10

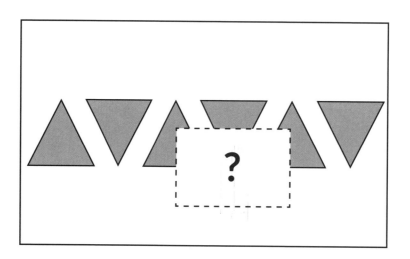

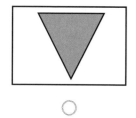   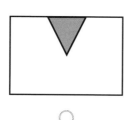   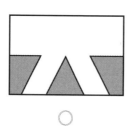   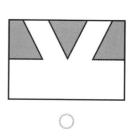   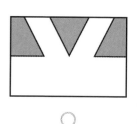

11

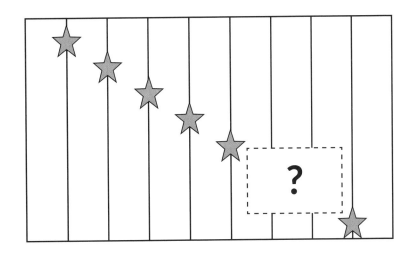

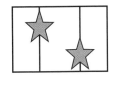

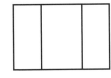

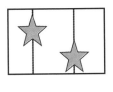

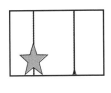

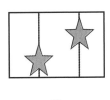

○   ○   ○   ○   ○

12

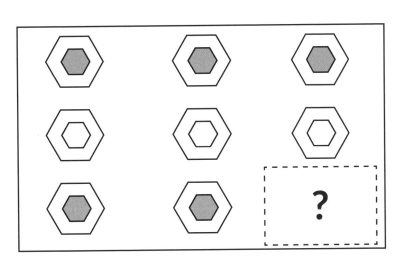

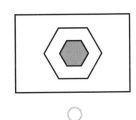

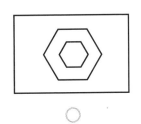

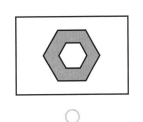

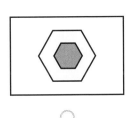

○   ○   ○   ○   ○

13

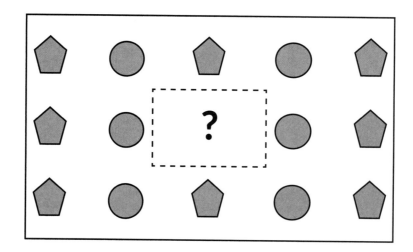

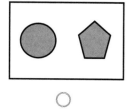

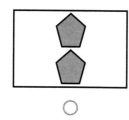

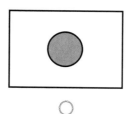

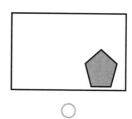

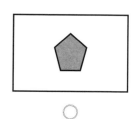

○   ○   ○   ○   ○

14

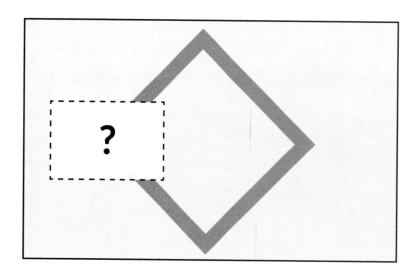

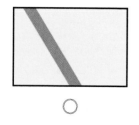

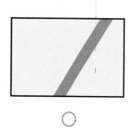

○   ○   ○   ○   ○

15

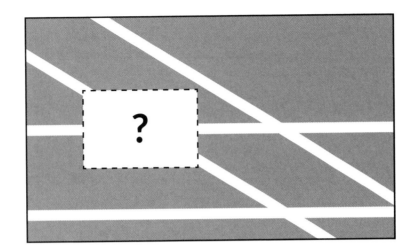

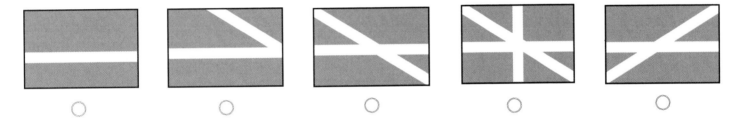

16

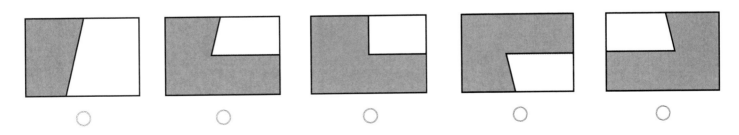

17

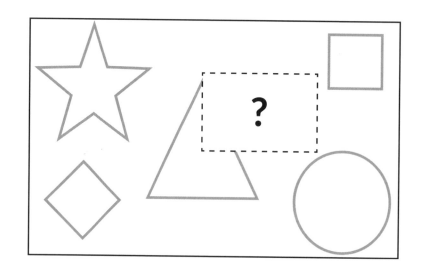

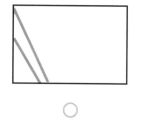 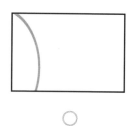 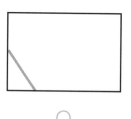 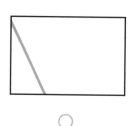 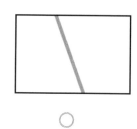

○ ○ ○ ○ ○

18

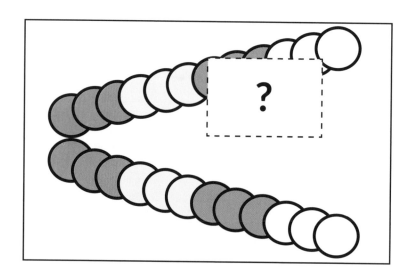

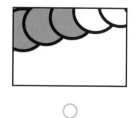 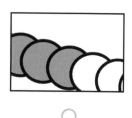 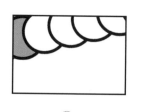 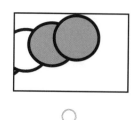 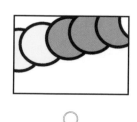

○ ○ ○ ○ ○

19

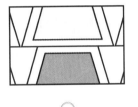 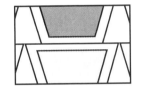 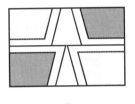 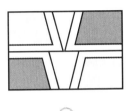 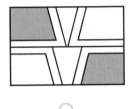

○ ○ ○ ○ ○

20

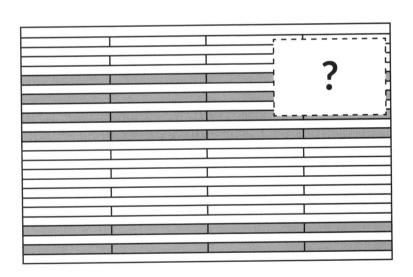

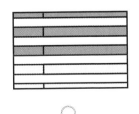 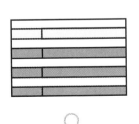 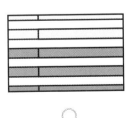 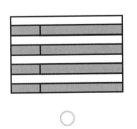 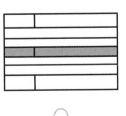

○ ○ ○ ○ ○

21

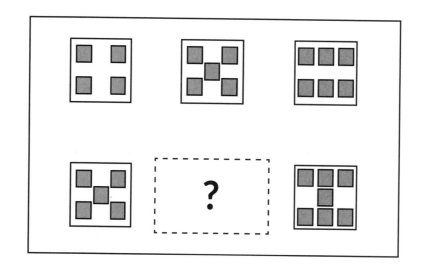

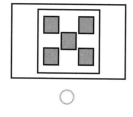

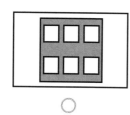

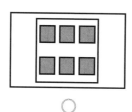

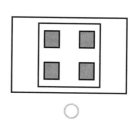

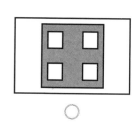

○   ○   ○   ○   ○

22

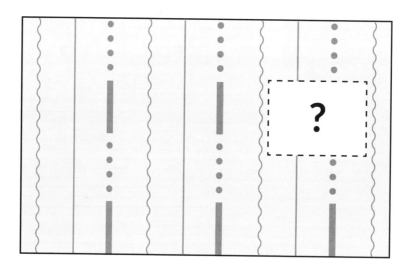

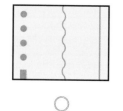

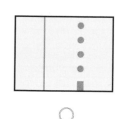

○   ○   ○   ○   ○

23

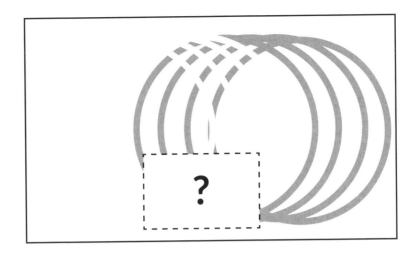

○ ○ ○ ○ ○

24

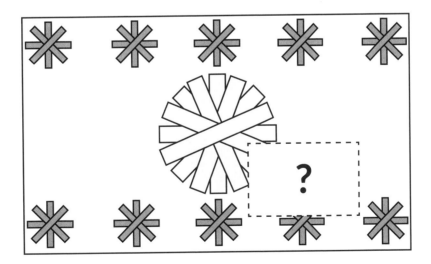

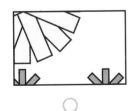 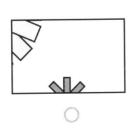 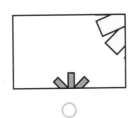 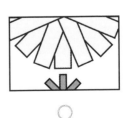 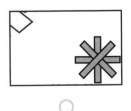

○ ○ ○ ○ ○

25

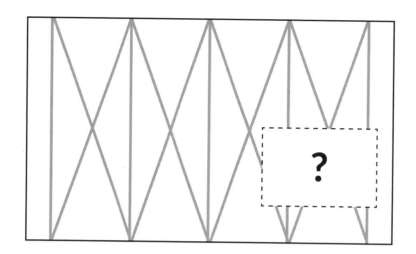

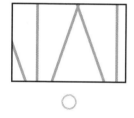 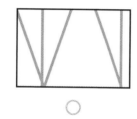 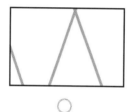 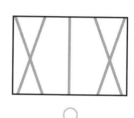 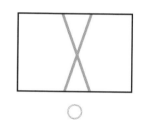

26

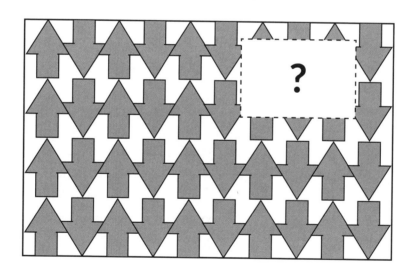

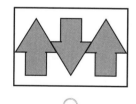 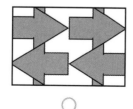 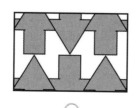 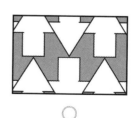 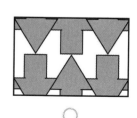

27

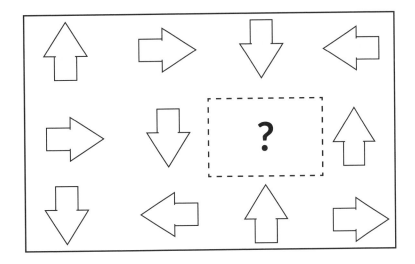

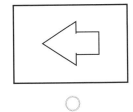 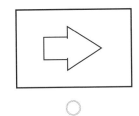 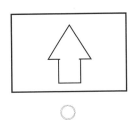 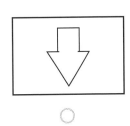 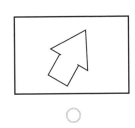

28

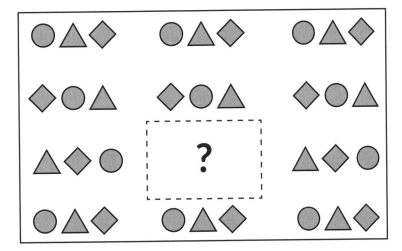

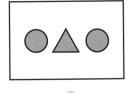 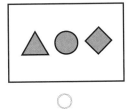 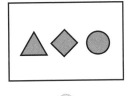 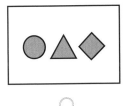 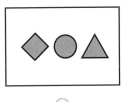

29

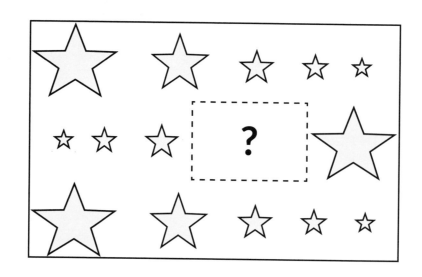

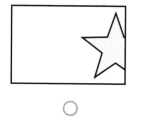 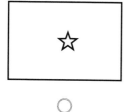   

○ ○ ○ ○ ○

30

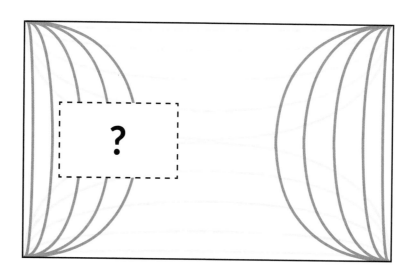

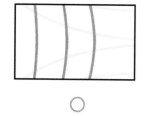 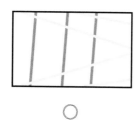 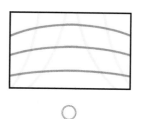 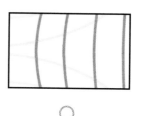 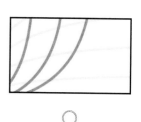

○ ○ ○ ○ ○

31

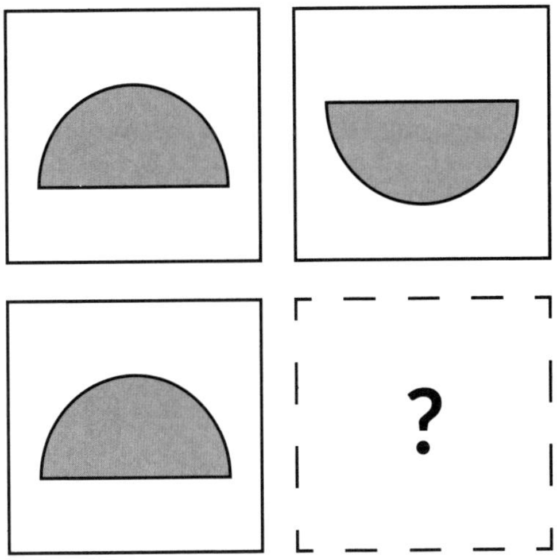

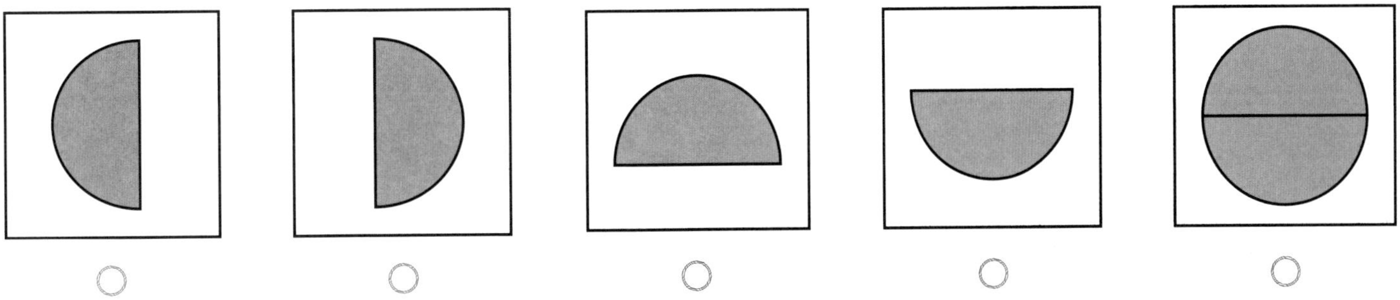

?

○   ○   ○   ○   ○

32

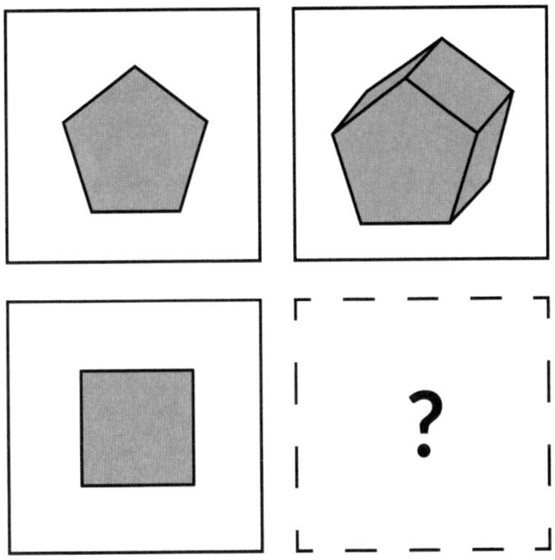

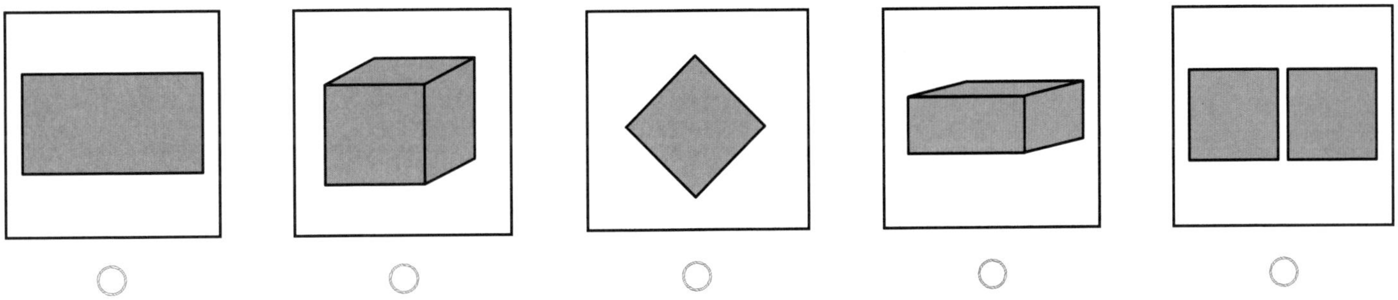

?

○   ○   ○   ○   ○

33

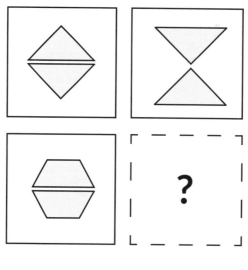

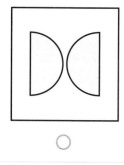 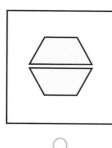 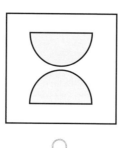 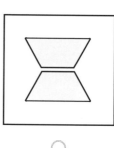 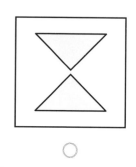

○   ○   ○   ○   ○

34

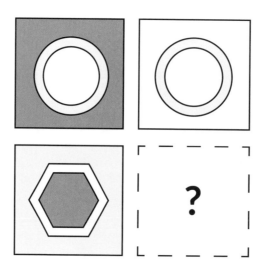

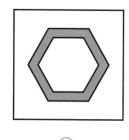 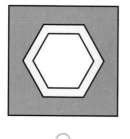 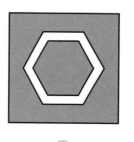 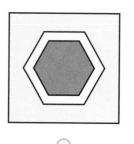 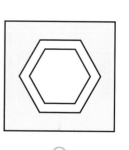

○   ○   ○   ○   ○

35

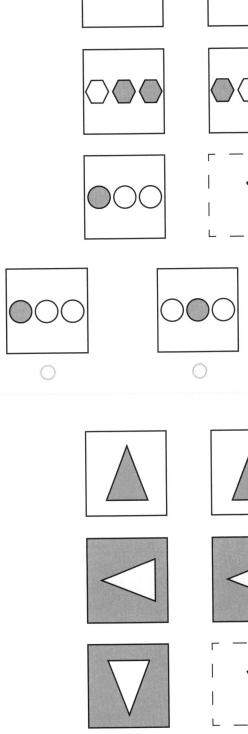

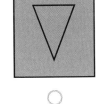

36

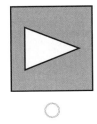

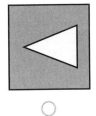

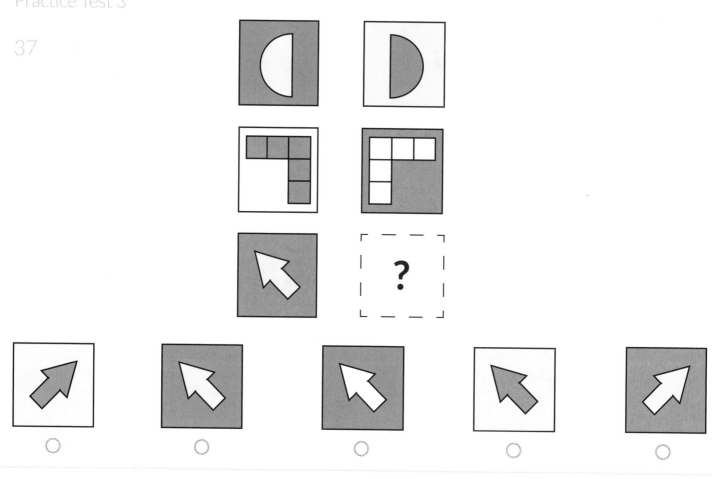

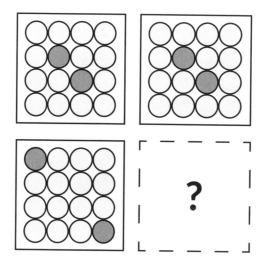

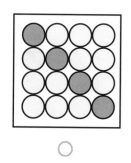

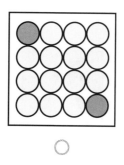

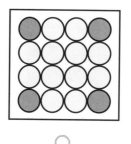

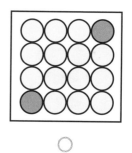

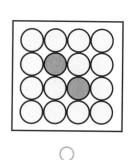

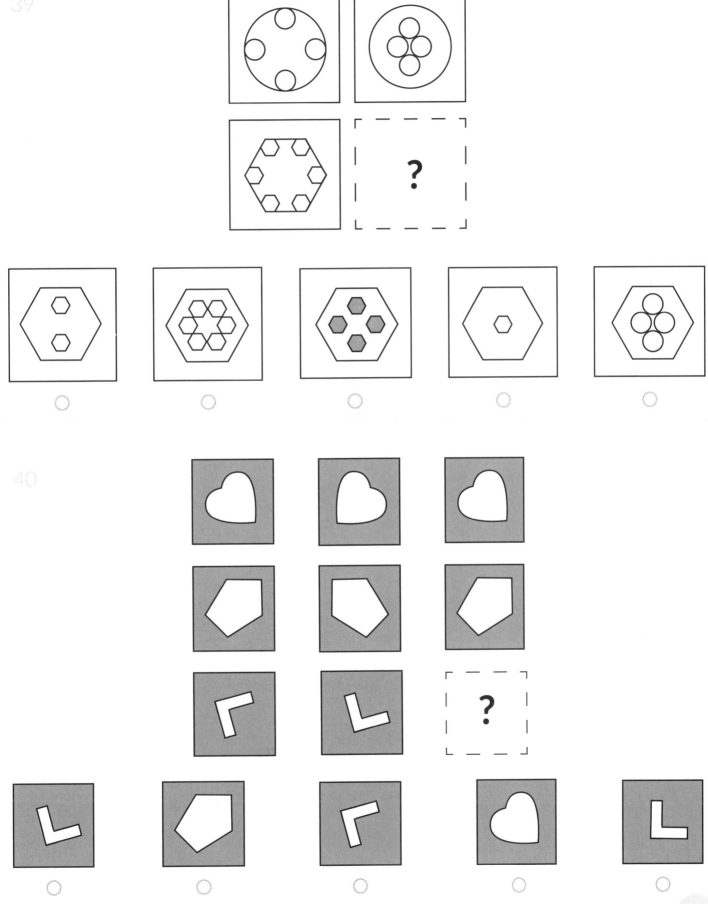

41

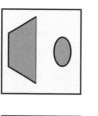 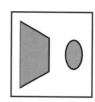

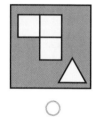 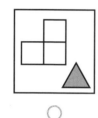 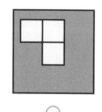 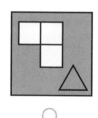 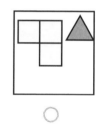

○ ○ ○ ○ ○

42

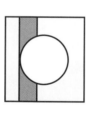 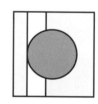

 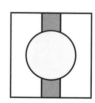

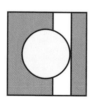

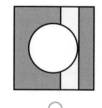 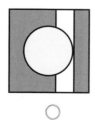 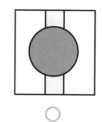 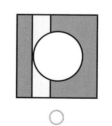 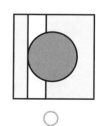

○ ○ ○ ○ ○

43

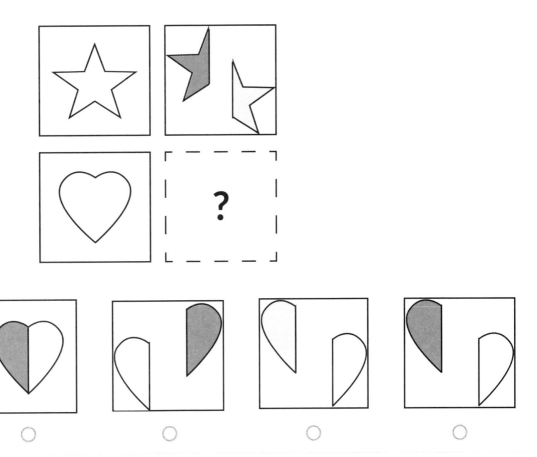

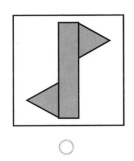   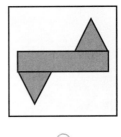 

○　　　　○　　　　○　　　　○　　　　○

44

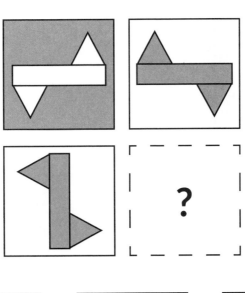

○　　　　○　　　　○　　　　○　　　　○

45

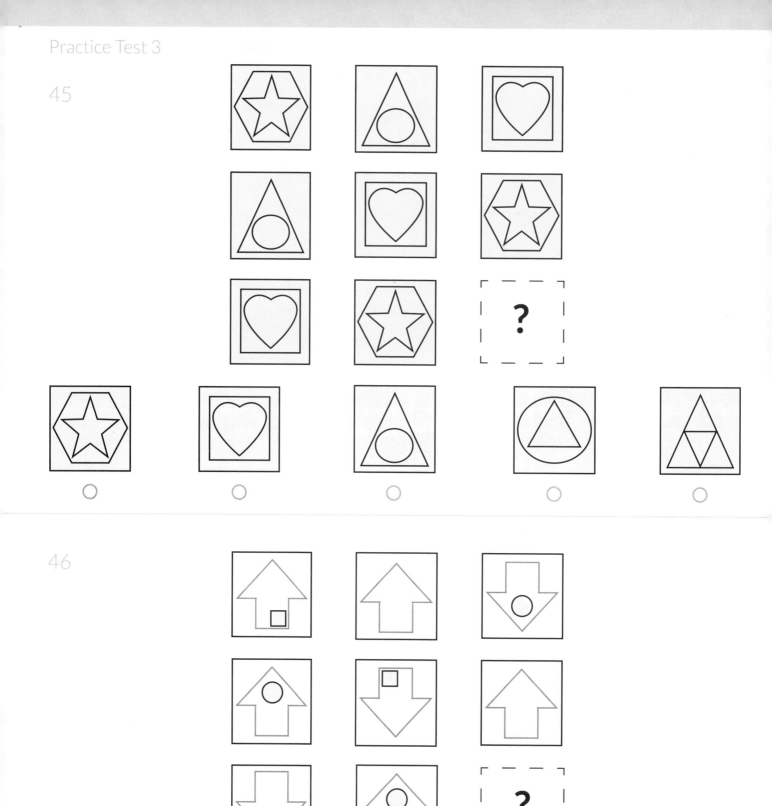

46

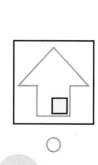
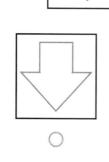

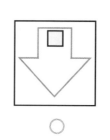
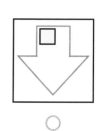

47

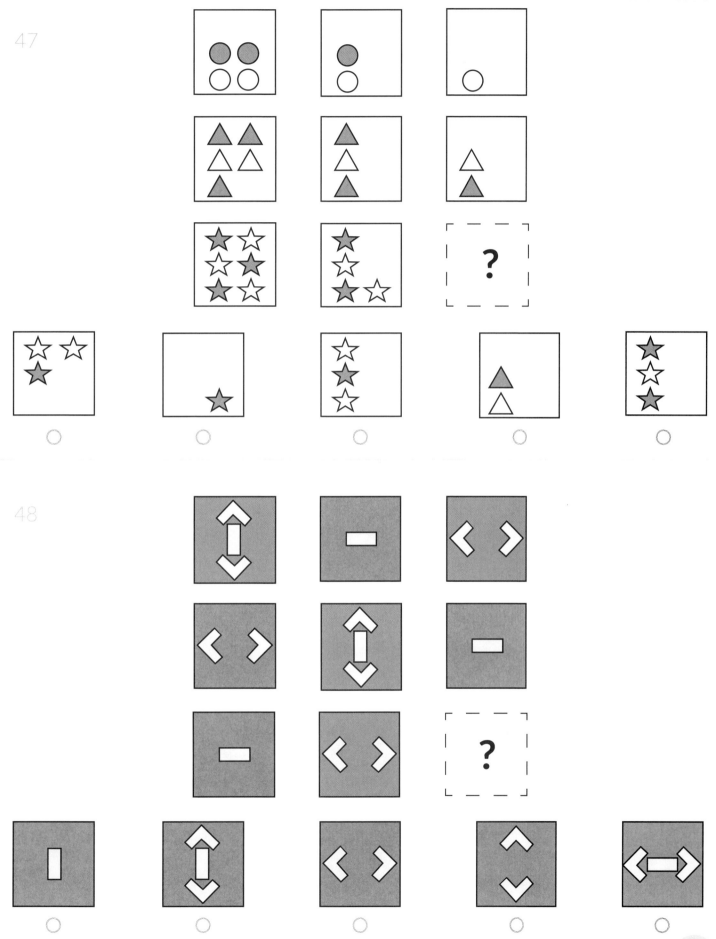

48

49

50

- End of Practice Test 3-

The Directions & Answer Keys begin on the next page.
Please cut out pages **92-94.**
Use pages **92-94** to check Practice Test answers.

PRACTICE TEST DIRECTIONS AND ANSWER KEYS

<u>IMPORTANT NOTES</u> If you wish to assign a time limit to mimic an actual test, allow approximately 30 minutes per test.

Directions for each question type are below in each question type's section. Each of the question types (Pattern Completion, Reasoning By Analogy, Serial Reasoning) have the same directions for all the questions of that question type. You do not need to repeat the directions for each question. If your child will take Level A, remember that Serial Reasoning questions are "challenge questions" for Level A and should be done with an adult.

Your child should fill in the answer "bubble" below his/her answer. The correct answers and space to write your child's answer are next to the question number. At the end of each section, total the number answered correctly. This will give an overview of your child's strengths / weaknesses relating to question type.

Additional explanations are provided for the Reasoning By Analogy and Serial Reasoning question types. As most of the Pattern Completion answers are self-explanatory (requiring test-takers to examine the composition of the picture's elements, especially those surrounding the question box), only some of the Pattern Completion questions have additional explanations.

<u>PRACTICE TEST 1, PATTERN COMPLETION</u>   Directions: Here is a puzzle where a piece is missing. (Point to the box with the question mark.) Which one of the answer choices would go here?

1.E _____   2.D _____   3.B _____

4.C _____   (Note the kind of shape and the shape color that appear in the pattern.)   5.A _____

6.B _____   7.E _____   (Note the width, quantity, and type of the yellow lines.)

8.D _____   9.C _____   (Note the quantity of each shape in the rows and how they get smaller.)

10.E _____   11.A _____   12.B _____

13.E _____   (Note the quantity of the correct answer: 4 stars - not 2 stars.)

14.D _____   (Note the direction of the lines and the width.)

15.D _____   (Note the appearance of the overall shape. Look at the green line on the other sides of the shape. The green lines point outward. They are angled. They are not completely straight, nor are they rounded.)

16.C _____   17.E _____   (Note the quantity and thickness of the white lines.)   18.A _____

19.B _____   (Note the three figures are the same.)   20.C _____   (Note the amount of space between the 2 lines.)

21.E _____   22.D _____   (Note pattern of the yellow shapes around the blue diamond: circle-hexagon-circle.)

23.E _____   (Note the box color pattern.)

24.B _____   (Note the pattern of the vertical lines: straight-curved-curved-straight-curved-curved.)

25.A _____   26.D _____   27.C _____   28.B _____   29.B _____

30.E _____   (Note the horizontal pattern of the arrows: pointing up – pointing right –pointing up – pointing right.)

Pattern Completion Questions Answered Correctly: _____ out of 30

<u>PRACTICE TEST 1, REASONING BY ANALOGY</u>   Directions: Look at the pictures inside the boxes on the top row. They go together in some way. On the bottom row, one box is missing. (Point to the question mark.) Look at the answer choices. Which one would go here?

31.E _____   (Yellow becomes green.)   32.B _____   (White becomes stripes.)

33.E _____   (Same.)   34.D _____   (Same line type on top, and same line type on bottom.)

35.A _____   (The diamond becomes a heart, and the heart becomes a diamond.)

36.C _____   (The shape gets larger.)   37.A _____   (Flips.)

38.C _____   (Gets larger & becomes blue.)   39.C _____   (One more shape is added.)

40.A _____   (Blue becomes yellow, and yellow becomes blue.)

41.E _____   (Flips. Or, white becomes blue, and blue becomes white.)

42.C _____   (The dotted line becomes a solid line and stays in the same location within the square.)

43.B _____   (The figures inside square flip, the figures and squares reverse color.)   44.C _____   (One more star is added.)

Reasoning by Analogy Questions Answered Correctly: _____ out of 14

<u>PRACTICE TEST 1, SERIAL REASONING</u>   Directions: Look at the pictures inside the boxes. They go together in some way. On the bottom, one box is missing. (Point to the question mark.) Look at the answer choices. Which one would go here?

45.B _____   (Every column and row must have an octagon, a star, and a trapezoid. Every row and column have a small shape, medium shape, and large shape.)

46.D _____   (In each row, the elements in the first square and second square come together to form elements in the third square. The same is true with each column. The elements of the first two squares come together to form elements in the third square.)

47.C _____   (Look at the overall image–it's symmetrical. The answer must have the missing piece to complete the blue circle.)

48.E _____   (In the rows and columns, the box colors switch between green and blue. Also, each row and column have a "wand" that points three different directions: right, left, up.)

49.A _____ (Across the rows and down the columns, the number of stars decreases by 1.)
50.D _____ (Each column and row have a pentagon, a star, and a pentagon + star together. Down the columns, the pentagon and the star remain the same color when they come together. For example, in column 1, the blue pentagon and the white star are together in the middle box. However, across the rows, the pentagon and the star switch colors. As another example, in row 1 the blue pentagon and the yellow star come together in the third box and switch colors. In the third row, the color of the pentagon must switch. However, in the third column, the color of the pentagon will remain the same: yellow.)

Serial Reasoning Questions Answered Correctly: _____ out of 6

PRACTICE TEST 2, PATTERN COMPLETION   Directions: Here is a puzzle where a piece is missing. (Point to the box with the question mark.) Which one of the answer choices would go here?

1.B _____   2.C _____   3.A _____   4.E _____   5.C _____
6.D _____   7.A _____   8.C _____   9.B _____   10.E _____
11.C _____   12.A _____   13.E _____   14.A _____   15.B _____
16.D _____   17.D _____ (Note the color pattern of the triangles: yellow – green – yellow.)
18.A _____   19.B _____ (Note the color pattern of the circles: 1 blue – 3 white – 1 blue.)
20.E _____
21.C _____   (Note the color pattern of the circles: yellow and white; both white; white and yellow. Also, note the position of the blue lines.)   22.B _____
23.A _____   (Note the pattern of the white and yellow boxes across the rows and down the columns.)
24.D _____   25.C _____
26.B _____   (Note the number of green circles and their part that is missing.)
27.E _____   28.B _____
29.A _____   (Note the number of blue lines needed to form the vertical and horizontal ovals and the correct spacing.)
30.C _____

Pattern Completion Questions Answered Correctly: _____ out of 30

PRACTICE TEST 2, REASONING BY ANALOGY   Directions: Look at the pictures inside the top boxes. They go together in some way. On the bottom row, one box is missing. (Point to the question mark.) Look at the answer choices. Which one would go here?

31.B _____   (Whole shape > half shape)
32.E _____   (Flips. Or, the order of shapes reverse and the shapes remain the same size.)
33.D _____   (The shapes increase by 1.)   34.B _____   (Lower half is covered in white.)
35.C _____   (Add one green side.)   36.A _____   (Flips.)
37.D _____   (Alternates; yellow-blue-yellow on top; white-wavy lines-white on bottom)
38.E _____   (The picture overall is symmetrical. The answer completes the blue and yellow figure. Or, the figure flips.)
39.C _____   (Small shape > larger version of same shape with borders that would be just outside of the white box)
40.D _____   (Flips. Or, the colors of the boxes & the colors of the circles switch.)
41.A _____   (Across the rows the number of shapes decreases by 1.)
42.B _____   (Same.)   43.C _____   (Shape turns slightly (45 degrees) to the right.)
44.E _____   (Shapes have the same number of sides: 4 on top, 8 on bottom.)

Reasoning by Analogy Questions Answered Correctly: _____ out of 14

PRACTICE TEST 2, SERIAL REASONING   Directions: Look at these pictures inside the boxes. They go together in some way. On the bottom, one box is missing. (Point to the question mark.) Look at the answer choices. Which one would go here?

45.D _____   (Across the rows, all boxes will have 1 horizontal line. Also, 1 box will have 1 vertical line and 2 boxes will have 2 vertical lines. Down the columns, the same is true - all boxes will have 1 horizontal line. Also, 1 box will have 1 vertical line and 2 boxes will have 2 vertical lines.)
46.D _____   (Each row will have the same 3 shapes with the same color box. Down the columns, the same shape appears with the same color pattern of the boxes: white-blue-yellow.)
47.A _____   (Across the rows and down the columns, the shapes in the first box and the second box combine to form the final box. Note that they are the same type of shape and they are in the same location as the first two boxes.)
48.C _____   (The "wands" all point inward respective to their location. For example, the "wand" in the top right box points inward from the upper right, the one just below points inward from the right, and the one missing points inward from the bottom right.)
49.B _____   (Across the rows, the shapes filled in with green in the first box and the shapes filled in with green in the second box combine to form the final box.)
50.E _____   (Across the rows, the figure first rotates 180°, then rotates clockwise by 90°.)

Serial Reasoning Questions Answered Correctly: _____ out of 6

PRACTICE TEST 3, PATTERN COMPLETION
Directions: Here is a puzzle where a piece is missing. (Point to the box with the question mark.) Which one of the answer choices would go here?

1.B _____   2.A _____   3.D _____

4.E _____   (Note the pattern of the shapes: hearts on the bottom row and heart-diamond-heart in last column.)

5.C _____   6.D _____   7.A _____   8.B _____   9.B _____

10.E _____   (Note the pattern of the blue triangles and the direction they are pointing.)   11.C _____

12.A _____   13.E _____   (Note pattern of the shapes.)   14.D _____   15.C _____

16.B _____   17.D _____   18.A _____   19.E _____   20.C _____

21.C _____   (Across the rows and down the columns, the number of blue squares increases by 1.)

22.D _____   (Note the pattern of the vertical line with dots: 4 dots–solid line –4 dots–solid line. The box covers 1 of the dots and a solid line. There's a solid line to the left.)

23.B _____   24.B _____   (Note number of stars' blue lines and large star's yellow lines.)

25.A _____   (Note number of green lines.)   26.C _____   (Note arrow pattern across rows: up-down-up-down.)

27.A _____   (Each row has an arrow pointing up, down, left, and right.)

28.C _____   (Note pattern of the shapes across the rows. The shapes are in the same order across the rows. Across the third row, the pattern is: triangle – diamond – circle.)

29.E _____   (Note number of stars in each row (5) and how they increase/decrease in size.)

30.A _____   (Note number of blue and yellow lines and their direction.)

Pattern Completion Questions Answered Correctly: _____ out of 30

PRACTICE TEST 3, REASONING BY ANALOGY
Directions: Look at the pictures inside the boxes on the top row. They go together in some way. On the bottom row, one box is missing. (Point to the question mark.) Look at the answer choices. Which one would go here?

31.D _____   (Flips.)   32.B _____   (Shape becomes 3-D/solid.)

33.D _____   (Two halves of shape flip to face each other.)

34.C _____   (The shape stays the same in top row (smaller white circle inside a larger yellow one) and the bottom row (smaller blue hexagon inside a larger white one). The background changes color.)

35.C _____   (In each of the three rows, the colors change in this way: yellow becomes white; blue becomes yellow; white becomes blue.)

36.E _____   (Same.)   37.A _____   (The shapes inside boxes flip. The colors of shape & colors of boxes reverse.)

38.B _____   (Same.)   39.B _____   (The group of smaller shapes inside larger shape moves toward the center.)

40.C _____   (Across the rows, the shape first flips and then goes back to its original position.)

41.D _____   (With the 2 shapes inside each set of boxes, the larger of the 2 shapes flips, while the smaller one stays in the same place. Both shapes stay the same color. The color of the boxes must change.)

42.A _____   (The color of the vertical line and circle switch. The color of the box and location of the vertical line stay the same in the set.)

43.E _____   (The shape splits in half. The left side is higher than the right side. Neither of the two halves is the same color as the whole shape from the first box.)

44.B _____   (The figure flips and reverses color.)

Reasoning by Analogy Questions Answered Correctly: _____ out of 14

PRACTICE TEST 3, SERIAL REASONING
Directions: Look at the pictures inside the boxes. They go together in some way. On the bottom, one box is missing. Look at the answer choices. Which one would go in the box with the question mark?

45.C _____   (The same 3 groups of 2 shapes appear across the rows and down the columns: hexagon with star inside, triangle with circle inside, square with heart inside.)

46.A _____   (Across the rows and down the columns 3 kinds of arrows appear: an arrow with a yellow square, an arrow with a yellow circle, and an arrow by itself. Also, each row and column have 1 arrow that points down and 2 arrows that point up.)

47.E _____   (Across the rows, 2 shapes are taken away, then 1 shape is taken away.)

48.B _____   (Each row and each column will have the parts of a horizontal arrow and of a complete vertical arrow. For example, the first row has a vertical arrow in the first box. The second box has the middle section of a horizontal arrow. The third box has the end points of a horizontal arrow. The last row/column is missing a complete vertical arrow.)

49.D _____   (Across the rows, the hexagon changes position in the middle box and then returns to its original position. Row 1: upper left – lower right – upper left. Row 2: lower right – upper left – lower right. Row 3: upper left – lower right – upper left. There is one green triangle. It rotates clockwise.)

50.C _____   (Each row/column has a circle, an oval pointed sideways, and an octagon. The first row has small shapes, the second row has medium shapes, and the third row has large shapes. Down the columns, the order of the shapes is small – medium – large.)

Serial Reasoning Questions Answered Correctly: _____ out of 6

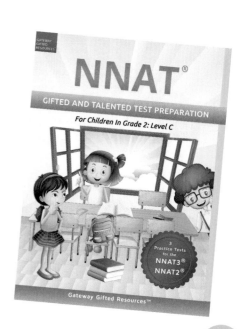

The Shape Detectives

Congratulations to:

_____

Our Newest Member!

PLEASE LEAVE US A REVIEW!

We are a family-owned publishing company - a consortium of educators, book designers, parents, and kid-testers. We would be thrilled if you left us a review on the site where you found this book!